RETHINKING HOMEWORK

2nd Edition

Another ASCD book by Cathy Vatterott:

*Rethinking Grading: Meaningful Assessment
for Standards-Based Learning*

Cathy Vatterott

*

RETHINKING HOMEWORK

Best Practices That Support Diverse Needs

2nd Edition

ASCD

Alexandria, VA USA

1703 N. Beauregard St. • Alexandria, VA 22311-1714 USA
Phone: 800-933-2723 or 703-578-9600 • Fax: 703-575-5400
Website: www.ascd.org • E-mail: member@ascd.org
Author guidelines: www.ascd.org/write

Deborah S. Delisle, *Executive Director;* Stefani Roth, *Publisher;* Genny Ostertag, *Director, Content Acquisitions;* Julie Houtz, *Director, Book Editing & Production;* Miriam Calderone, *Editor;* Judi Connelly, *Associate Art Director;* Georgia Park, *Senior Graphic Designer;* Keith Demmons, *Production Designer;* Mike Kalyan, *Director, Production Services;* Trinay Blake, *E-Publishing Specialist;* Dirk Cassard, *Production Specialist*

All web links in this book are correct as of the publication date below but may have become inactive or otherwise modified since that time. If you notice a deactivated or changed link, please e-mail books@ascd.org with the words "Link Update" in the subject line. In your message, please specify the web link, the book title, and the page number on which the link appears.

PAPERBACK ISBN: 978-1-4166-2656-5   ASCD product #119001   n9/18
PDF E-BOOK ISBN: 978-1-4166-2658-9; see Books in Print for other formats.
Quantity discounts are available: e-mail programteam@ascd.org or call 800-933-2723, ext. 5773, or 703-575-5773. For desk copies, go to www.ascd.org/deskcopy.

Library of Congress Cataloging-in-Publication Data

Names: Vatterott, Cathy, 1951- author. | Association for Supervision and
  Curriculum Development.
Title: Rethinking homework : best practices that support diverse needs /
  Cathy Vatterott.
Description: Updated Second Edition. | Alexandria, Virginia : ASCD, [2018] |
  Previous edition: 2009. | Includes bibliographical references and index.
Identifiers: LCCN 2018025740 (print) | LCCN 2018027067 (ebook) | ISBN
  9781416626589 (PDF) | ISBN 9781416626565 (paperback)
Subjects: LCSH: Homework. | Motivation in education.
Classification: LCC LB1048 (ebook) | LCC LB1048 .V37 2018 (print) | DDC
  371.3/0281—dc23
LC record available at https://lccn.loc.gov/2018025740

27 26 25 24 23 22 21 20 19 18   1 2 3 4 5 6 7 8 9 10 11 12

To the children

~

May their backpacks be light and
their learning joyful.

RETHINKING HOMEWORK

Best Practices That Support Diverse Needs

2nd Edition

Acknowledgments

My thanks go first to ASCD for an educational vision that has guided my career and for the forum it has provided for my ideas. I am honored to be an ASCD author. I also wish to thank Genny Ostertag, who first encouraged me to write this second edition, knowledgeably pointed me to the best and newest related research, and gently guided me back on track when my creative brain diverged down various rabbit holes. She served as my editor, cheerleader, and taskmaster, and she smoothed the rough edges from some of my most passionate rants. Thanks also to Miriam Calderone for her thoughtful suggestions and her meticulous attention to detail.

My special thanks go to five authors who started and refined the conversation about homework and helped to guide my work.

The first of these authors are Etta Kralovec and John Buell, whose groundbreaking book *The End of Homework: How Homework Disrupts Families, Overburdens Children, and Limits Learning* (2000) dared to question an entrenched practice and first gave me comfort that I was not alone in my concerns.

Next, thanks to Alfie Kohn, whose numerous writings and presentations have greatly influenced my work. More than any other author, Alfie challenged me to think outside the box, to question the status quo, and to be irreverent without apology. His book *The Homework Myth: Why Our Kids Get Too Much of a*

Bad Thing (2006) critiqued the beliefs and norms about home-work that we take for granted and proved to be great inspiration for my ideas.

I also owe thanks to Sara Bennett and Nancy Kalish, whose book *The Case Against Homework: How Homework Is Hurting Our Children and What We Can Do About It* (2006) poignantly shared the homework dilemmas of families and galvanized a parental movement for reasonable homework. Their book lent voice and dignity to the parent's perspective and legitimized the right of parents to be part of the homework discussion.

Etta, Alfie, and Sara were never too busy to talk to me and to share their thoughts and resources. Their support was unyield-ing and their insights invaluable in the shaping of my ideas. I thank them for validating my "crusade" to reform homework practices.

Most recently, I also owe thanks to authors Denise Pope and Vicki Abeles, who sounded the alarm about the over-the-top stress levels of many of our students and exposed the role of homework in exacerbating that stress.

This book would not be the same without the questions, insights, and examples provided by thousands of teachers, administrators, and parents who attended my workshops and institutes during the last 20 years. Their questions challenged my ideas, their reflections caused me to rethink, and the examples they shared from their classrooms and schools made it all real. The quotes and examples shared in this book came from those brief encounters as well as from more in-depth discussions with other teachers and administrators. I have learned so much from all of them.

I am also grateful to journalists, often parents of school-age children themselves, who made the homework research acces-sible to the public and who wrote passionately about their own homework struggles. Over the years, they have provided an unrelenting voice to the concerns of parents from all corners of the world and from all stations in life.

Many other people contributed to this book. I had numerous conversations with friends, families, and other parents (sometimes strangers on a plane), all anxious to share their opinions and personal stories about homework. I have never tired of those discussions—it's been great fun.

Thanks also to my husband Glenn, who for 20 years has patiently endured long conversations about homework at parties, family gatherings, and social events, never once trying to change the subject.

And finally, I am grateful to my son Andrew, who started it all. His learning struggles in elementary school frustrated me as both a parent and an educator and were the driving force that first caused me to question the value of homework. Thanks to the dedication, creativity, and perseverance of his special education teachers, he survived and eventually thrived as a student. Watching Andrew grow first into a successful college student and now a successful adult has been one of the greatest joys and affirmations of my life. I wrote this book for other students like him.

Preface

Twenty years ago, when I was the totally frustrated parent of a 5th grader with learning disabilities, homework was a daily battle. I had an aching feeling that there was something wrong with homework, so I began looking at the research. My initial interest soon grew into an obsession and a passion to learn everything I could about this complicated issue. Who could have predicted where we are today—that some elementary schools would ban homework, that some schools would no longer count homework in the grade, and that some parents would begin to "just say no"? To quote the Grateful Dead, "What a long strange trip it's been." And what a gratifying one. I am proud to have been part of the movement.

Since the first edition of this book was published in 2009, much has changed, but the controversy surrounding homework has not abated. Research has still been unable to show proof of homework's benefit. Parents and teachers alike still confuse homework load with rigor and compliance with responsibility. More recently, media discussions have focused on elementary schools that are banning homework and parents who are becoming more vocal in their opinions.

Since 2009,

- The economic divide in the United States has widened, leading to increasing awareness of homework challenges for students living in poverty, often without Internet access, known as the "homework gap" or "digital divide."

- Research about the learning process has shown the importance of
  - Formative feedback.
  - A growth mindset.
  - Brain research about factors influencing learning.
  - Sleep and downtime.

- Educational trends are changing the role of homework in the teaching and learning process:
  - With the move toward standards-based learning and standards-based grading, homework is increasingly viewed as ungraded formative assessment.
  - Educators have come to appreciate the motivational role of personalized learning, choice, and student self-assessment.
  - The increased use of flipped learning has caused the homework task itself to change.

- There has been an increase in the number of K–12 school policies limiting or eliminating homework at the elementary level.
- There has been an increase in the number of K–12 school policies limiting the percentage homework may count in the grade or prohibiting teachers from counting homework in the grade.
- We have evolved from a time when homework was assigned as tradition, with little thought given to how the task related to the ultimate learning outcome, to a time when its basic value to learning is questioned.
- We have gone from the norm of vague or nonexistent homework policies to the norm of homework policies outlining the purpose and amount of homework and sometimes banning weekend or holiday homework.

- As our knowledge of the brain has grown, we have come to value the role of feedback and respect the power of student mindset and attitude.
- As the pace of our culture has accelerated at warp speed, we have become increasingly concerned about the role homework plays in the stress levels of K–12 students. We have begun to understand the importance of balancing work, play, downtime, and sleep to ensure the efficient functioning of a learning brain and the mental health of our children.
- These concerns about "academic stress" and work-life balance for students have contributed to increasing parent activism about homework.

We have moved from blind acceptance of homework, to awareness and questioning of the practice, to understanding and advocacy for what is best for our students. May we continue to study, learn, reflect, and improve our practice of homework.

The Cult(ure) of Homework

Homework is a long-standing education tradition that, until recently, has seldom been questioned. The concept of homework has become so ingrained in U.S. culture that the word *homework* is part of the common vernacular, as exemplified by statements such as "Do your homework before taking a trip," "It's obvious they didn't do their homework before they presented their proposal," and "The marriage counselor gave us homework to do."

Homework began generations ago, when schooling consisted primarily of reading, writing, and arithmetic, and rote learning dominated. Simple tasks of memorization and practice were easy for children to do at home, and the belief was that such mental exercise disciplined the mind. Homework has generally been viewed as a positive practice and accepted without question as part of the student routine. But over the years, homework in U.S. schools has evolved from the once simple tasks of memorizing math facts or writing spelling words to complex projects.

As the culture has changed, and as schools and families have changed, homework has become problematic for more and more students, parents, and teachers. The Internet and bookstores are crowded with books offering parents advice on how to get children to do homework. Frequently, the advice for parents is to "remain positive," yet only a handful of books suggest that parents should have the right to question the amount of homework or the value of the task itself. Teachers, overwhelmed by an already glutted curriculum and pressures related to standardized tests, assign homework in an attempt to develop students' skills and extend learning time. At the same time, they are left frustrated when the students who most need more time to learn seem the least likely to complete homework. Teachers are afraid not to give homework for fear of being perceived as "easy."

Despite there being more diversity among learners in our schools than ever, many teachers continue to assign the same homework to all students in the class and continue to disproportionately fail students from lower-income households for not doing homework, in essence punishing them for lack of an adequate environment in which to do homework. At a time when demand for accountability has reached a new high, research fails to prove that homework is worth all that trouble. (The research on homework is discussed in Chapter 3.)

Although many people remain staunchly in favor of homework, a growing number of teachers and parents alike are beginning to question the practice. These critics are reexamining the beliefs behind the practice, the wisdom of assigning hours of homework, the absurdly heavy backpack, and the failure that can result when some students don't complete homework. There's a growing suspicion that something is wrong with homework.

This more critical view represents a movement away from the pro-homework attitudes that have been consistent for decades (Kralovec & Buell, 2000). As a result, a discussion of homework stirs controversy as people debate both sides of the issue. But the arguments both for and against homework are not new, as indicated by a consistent swing of the pendulum over the last 100 years between pro-homework and anti-homework attitudes.

A Brief History of Homework

The history of homework and surrounding attitudes is relevant because the roots of homework dogma developed and became entrenched over the last 100 years. Attitudes toward homework have historically reflected societal trends and the prevailing educational philosophy of the time, and each swing of the pendulum is colored by unique historical events and sentiments that drove the movement for or against homework. Yet the historical arguments on both sides are familiar. They bear a striking similarity to the arguments waged in today's debate over homework.

At the end of the 19th century, attendance in grades 1 through 4 was irregular for many students, and most classrooms were multi-age. Teachers rarely gave homework to primary students (Gill & Schlossman, 2004). By the 5th grade, many students left school for work; fewer continued to high school (Kralovec & Buell, 2000). In the lower grades, school focused on reading, writing, and arithmetic; in grammar school (grades 5 through 8) and high school, students studied geography, history, literature, and math. Learning consisted of drill, memorization, and recitation, which required preparation at home:

> At a time when students were required to say their lessons in class in order to demonstrate their academic prowess, they had little alternative but to say those lessons over and over at home the night before. Before a child could continue his or her schooling through grammar school, a family had to decide that chores and other family obligations would not interfere unduly with the predictable nightly homework hours that would go into preparing the next day's lessons. (Gill & Schlossman, 2004, p. 174)

The critical role that children played as workers in the household meant that many families could not afford to have their children continue schooling, given the requisite two to three hours of homework each night (Kralovec & Buell, 2000).

Early in the 20th century, an anti-homework movement became the centerpiece of a nationwide trend toward progressive education. Progressive educators questioned many aspects of schooling: "Once the value of drill, memorization, and recitation was opened to debate, the attendant need for homework came under harsh scrutiny as well" (Kralovec & Buell, 2000, p. 42).

As the field of pediatrics grew, more doctors began to speak out about the effect of homework on the health and well-being of children. The benefits of fresh air, sunshine, and exercise for children were widely accepted, and homework had the potential to interfere. One hundred years ago, rather than diagnosing children with attention deficit disorder, pediatricians simply prescribed more outdoor exercise. Homework was blamed for nervous conditions in children, eyestrain, stress, lack of sleep, and other conditions. Homework was viewed as a culprit that robbed children of important opportunities for social interaction. At the same time, labor leaders were protesting working conditions for adults, advocating for a 40-hour workweek. Child labor laws were used as a justification to protect children from excessive homework.

In 1900, the editor of the *Ladies' Home Journal,* Edward Bok, began a series of anti-homework articles. He recommended the elimination of homework for all students under the age of 15 and a limit of one hour nightly for older students. His writings were instrumental in the growth of the anti-homework movement of the early 1900s, a harbinger of the important role media would play in future homework debates. By 1930, the anti-homework sentiment had grown so strong that a Society for the Abolition of Homework was formed. Many school districts across the United States voted to abolish homework, especially in the lower grades:

> In the 1930s and 1940s, although few districts abolished homework outright, many abolished it in grades K–6. In grades K–3, condemnation of homework was nearly universal in school district policies as well as professional opinion.

And even where homework was not abolished, it was often assigned only in small amounts—in secondary schools as well as elementary schools. (Gill & Schlossman, 2000, p. 32)

After the Soviet Union launched the *Sputnik 1* satellite in 1957, the trend toward less homework was quickly reversed as the United States became obsessed with competing with the Russians. Fearful that children were unprepared to compete in a future that would be increasingly dominated by technology, school officials, teachers, and parents saw homework as a means for accelerating children's acquisition of knowledge:

The homework problem was reconceived as part of a national crisis: the U.S. was losing the Cold War because Russian children were smarter; that is, they were working harder and achieving more in school . . . the new discourse pronounced too little homework an indicator of the dismal state of American schooling. A commitment to heavy homework loads was alleged to reveal seriousness of purpose in education; homework became an instrument of national defense policy. (Gill & Schlossman, 2004, p. 176)

Within a few short years, public opinion had swung back to the pro-homework position. During this period, many schools overturned policies abolishing or limiting homework that had been established between 1900 and 1940. However, homework in the early elementary grades was still rare (Gill & Schlossman, 2004).

By the late 1960s and early 1970s, in the midst of the Vietnam War and the civil rights movement, a counterculture emerged that questioned the status quo in literally every aspect of personal and political life. A popular book, *Teaching as a Subversive Activity* (Postman & Weingartner, 1969), attacked traditional methods of what was labeled "the educational establishment." Indicative of the times, a new debate emerged over homework and other educational activities. The anti-homework arguments were reminiscent of the progressive arguments of the early 20th century—again, homework was seen as a symptom of too much pressure on students to achieve.

Two prominent educational organizations went on record opposing excessive homework. The American Educational Research Association stated,

> Whenever homework crowds out social experience, outdoor recreation, and creative activities, and whenever it usurps time that should be devoted to sleep, it is not meeting the basic needs of children and adolescents. (In Wildman, 1968, p. 204)

The National Education Association issued this statement in 1966:

> It is generally recommended (a) that children in the early elementary school have no homework specifically assigned by the teacher; (b) that limited amounts of homework—not more than an hour a day—be introduced during the upper elementary school and junior high years; (c) that homework be limited to four nights a week; and (d) that in secondary school no more than one and a half hours a night be expected. (In Wildman, 1968, p. 204)

Not surprisingly, by the late 1960s and during the 1970s, parents were arguing that children should be free to play and relax in the evenings, and again the amount of homework decreased (Bennett & Kalish, 2006).

But by the 1980s the pendulum would swing again. In 1983, the study *A Nation at Risk* became the "first major report by the government attempting to prove that the purported inadequacies of our schools and our students were responsible for the troubles of the U.S. economy" (Kralovec & Buell, 2000, p. 50). The report claimed that there was a "rising tide of mediocrity" in schools and that a movement for academic excellence was needed (National Commission on Excellence in Education, 1983). *A Nation at Risk* planted the seed of the idea that school success was responsible for economic success. It ratcheted up the standards, starting what has been called the "intensification movement"—the idea that education can be improved if only there is more of it, in the form of longer school years, more testing, more homework. *A Nation at Risk* explicitly called for "far more homework" for high school students.

In 1986, the U.S. Department of Education published *What Works*, which also recommended homework as an effective learning strategy. "Whenever you come across a particularly savage attack on the state of public education, it's a safe bet that a call for more homework (and other get-tough messages) will be sounded as well" (Kohn, 2006, p. 120).

The pro-homework trend continued into the 1990s, as the push for higher standards resulted in the conclusion that more homework was a remedy. As noted earlier, this was not the first time homework became the scapegoat for the perceived inadequacies of public education:

> Whenever reformers attempt to improve the academic outcomes of American schooling, more homework seems a first step. The justification for this probably has more to do with philosophy (students should work harder) and with the ease of implementation (increased homework costs no extra money and requires no major program modifications) than with new research findings. (Strother, in Connors, 1991, p. 14)

During the late 1980s and the early 1990s, an occasional journal article would question whether more homework was necessarily better, but those voices were few and far between. Most journal articles and popular books about homework took the safe position of being pro-homework and focused on strategies for getting children to complete homework. In 1989,

Harris Cooper (now considered a leading expert on homework research) published an exhaustive synthesis of research on homework (1989a) that seemed to have little effect on popular practice and received little media attention. In 1994, a board member in the school district of Half Moon Bay, California, made national news by recommending that the district abolish homework. The board member "was widely vilified in the national press as just another California kook" (Gill & Schlossman, 1996, p. 57). The general media reaction was dismissive; the story was treated as cute and quirky, as if the idea of abolishing homework were just plain crazy.

By the late 1990s, however, the tide would turn against homework once more. With increasing frequency, articles critical of traditional homework practices were published in educational journals. In 1998, the American Educational Research Association conducted a symposium on homework practices. In 1998, Harris Cooper's latest research about homework (Cooper, Lindsay, Nye, & Greathouse, 1998) garnered much more public attention, catapulting the topic of homework into the popular press and landing him on *Oprah* and *Today*. In March 1998, the cover of *Newsweek* featured an article titled "Does Your Child Need a Tutor?" along with another article titled "Homework Doesn't Help" (Begley, 1998). In January 1999, *Time* magazine's cover story, "The Homework That Ate My Family" (Ratnesar, 1999), generated considerable media buzz. It portrayed homework as an intrusion on family tranquility and as just one more stressor in an already overstressed life, especially for two-career families. The article also cited a University of Michigan study showing that homework for 6- to 8-year-olds had increased by more than 50 percent from 1981 to 1997.

As homework increased, especially for the youngest students, and parents began feeling overwhelmed, stories detailing the struggle appeared widely in the popular press. Now the mood was one of concern for overworked students and parents.

In 2000, Piscataway, New Jersey, received national attention for implementing a homework policy that limited the amount of homework, discouraged weekend homework, and forbade teachers from counting homework in the grade (Kohn, 2006). Unlike the story about Half Moon Bay only six years earlier, *this* story was given serious media coverage, and the school district was deluged by requests from schools seeking a copy of the policy.

Also in 2000, Etta Kralovec and John Buell's book *The End of Homework: How Homework Disrupts Families, Overburdens Children, and Limits Learning* received massive media attention and spawned an ongoing debate between the anti-homework and pro-homework contingents. In 2006, two popular-press books kept the debate going: Alfie Kohn's *The Homework Myth: Why Our Kids Get Too Much of a Bad Thing,* and Sara Bennett and Nancy Kalish's *The Case Against Homework: How Homework Is Hurting Our Children and What We Can Do About It.*

Since the first edition of this book was published in 2009, the debate has continued, with a strong anti-homework movement emerging, similar to the anti-homework cycles of the 1930s and 1940s and the late 1960s to early 1970s. Canada and the United Kingdom were two of the earliest countries to sound the alarm: a ban on primary homework was recommended in the United Kingdom in 2009, and in 2010, Toronto's school policy prohibited homework in kindergarten and on weekends and holidays. Around the same time, a smattering of elementary schools in the United States began limiting or eliminating homework. More and more newspaper articles appeared questioning the value of homework: "Do Kids Today Have Too Much Homework?" (Lawrence, 2015), "Homework: Is There Any Point?" (Norton, 2013), "As Students Return to School, Debate About the Amount of Homework Rages" (Hauser, 2016). In 2013, a particularly influential article appeared in *The Atlantic*. Titled "My Daughter's Homework Is Killing Me," the piece chronicled one New York dad's experience doing his 8th grade daughter's homework for a week, about three hours of work each night (Greenfeld, 2013).

Internationally, concerns about homework, especially for elementary students, have arisen in many countries, including Ireland, the Philippines, Greece, France, India, Japan, Singapore, and Australia. Even the government of China, a country long revered as the paragon of educational achievement, has warned schools and parents that excessive homework is not in the best interest of their children's health.

In the United States, there has been a move to more precisely examine the practice, to reduce the amount of homework, and to question the validity and quality of the homework tasks we ask students to do. Although the loudest voices are calling for a ban, the more centrist voices are simply asking schools to assign homework more thoughtfully and to consider the broader effects excessive homework has on the well-being of students and their families. The most consistent trend in the United States has been the adoption of policies that either ban elementary school homework or limit it to reading. A small but growing number of U.S. elementary schools are now "homework free" (CBS News, 2016). The trend line is clear: momentum has shifted in the direction of the "less homework" movement.

But trends do not tell the whole story, and not everyone has "joined the church" of less homework. Among those opposed to homework reform, a rather simplistic view has arisen mislabeling today's reform efforts as flat-out anti-homework and claiming that there are only two positions on homework: for or against. Although this is clearly a false dichotomy, attempts by schools to diminish the homework load do often provoke kneejerk opposition and accusations of "dumbing down" our children's education. Those of us in favor of such reform are labeled whiners and slackers. The pro-homework forces continue to tout the virtues of homework, claiming that evidence of the negative effects of excessive homework is anecdotal and not indicative of a general problem, as with this headline from the *Dallas Morning News* (Floyd, 2016): "Sorry, Parents, Your Child Probably Doesn't Have Too Much Homework."

Like religion and politics, the arguments surrounding homework stir intense emotions among parents, teachers, and administrators. To fully understand today's debate, we must examine the beliefs about homework that have developed during the last 100 years and the cultural forces that have shaped them.

Five Beliefs That Lay Bare the Culture of Homework

Beliefs about the inherent goodness of homework are so entrenched, so unshakable for many parents and educators, that they seem almost cultlike. For many, these beliefs are unexamined. Kralovec and Buell (2000) said it best: "The belief in the value of homework is akin to faith" (p. 9). The true believers hold homework in such reverence that many educators are afraid to recommend eliminating it completely. Too many people just won't accept the idea. How can anyone be against *work*? It's as if the tradition of homework has been so romanticized as to be accepted as truth. Parenting magazines and newspaper articles accept without question that homework is part of school life and then continue to give advice on how to help kids complete it (Kohn, 2006). Freelance writers have learned that writing that is too anti-homework will probably not be published in the mainstream media.

To understand the *cult*ure of homework and how it developed over the last 100 years, it is necessary to dissect the dogma, which can best be summarized by five largely unexamined beliefs about children and learning. How many of these beliefs are based on fact, and how many are based on faith, tradition, or moral judgments?

Belief #1: The Role of the School Is to Extend Learning Beyond the Classroom

Many believe that it is not only teachers' inalienable right but also their *obligation* to extend learning beyond the classroom. Inherent in this belief is the assumption that teachers have the *right* to control children's lives outside the school—that we have the right to give homework and that students and parents should comply with our wishes (more about this assumption in Chapter 2). Many teachers claim that homework keeps children out of trouble and is better for them than television or video games. This view is rather dismissive of parents' ability to make good decisions about their children's use of free time. Is it really our job to be the morality police of our students' personal lives?

Perhaps our role in extending learning outside the school is to instill in students the value of learning and the joy of learning and to expose them to the vastness of the universe—how much there is to learn. Perhaps our role is to help students find something in life they feel passionate about and to help them find their purpose in society.

Belief #2: Intellectual Activity Is Intrinsically More Valuable Than Nonintellectual Activity

Many homework advocates believe that intellectual development is more important than social, emotional, or physical development. Intellectual pursuits hold an implied superiority over nonintellectual tasks such as throwing a ball, walking a dog, riding a bike, or just hanging out. This belief presupposes the limited value of leisure tasks. Concurrently, some worry that too much unstructured time might cause children to be less successful, less competitive with others. As with Belief #1, this view shows a distrust of parents to guide children in the productive use of free time and a distrust of children to engage in intellectual pursuits on their own. In reality, physical, emotional, and social activities are as necessary as intellectual activity in the development of healthy, well-rounded children.

Belief #3: Homework Teaches Responsibility

One of the most resilient beliefs is that homework promotes responsibility and discipline. Even though there is no research to support this belief, many people continue to tout homework's nonacademic virtues (Kohn, 2006). *Responsibility* is often a code word for *obedience*. When we say we want students to be *responsible,* are we saying we want them to be *obedient*—to do *what* we want them to do *when* we want them to do it, to be mindless drones, blindly obedient to authority? One teacher said she thought not doing homework was a sign of disrespect for the teacher! When we say homework promotes discipline in students, does that mean being self-disciplined enough to do something they hate to do because it's their duty?

Many teachers are fixated on homework as *the way* to teach responsibility, as though we have no other avenues. We tend to neglect all the other ways students *could* be given responsibility in the classroom—involving them in decision making about their learning, teaching them how to self-assess, letting them design learning tasks, or allowing them to help manage classroom and school facilities (Guskey & Anderman, 2008; Vatterott, 2007). Even in the task of homework itself, children are rarely given *responsibility* for choosing how they wish to learn, how they might show what they have learned, or how they might schedule their time for homework. True responsibility cannot be coerced. It must be developed by giving students power and ownership of tasks (Anderson, 2016; Azzam, 2014; Vatterott, 2007). (Chapter 4 presents more about how to do this.)

Another supposed virtue of homework is that it teaches time management. Does time management really mean the ability to delay gratification—to work when we want to play? Homework does not reinforce time management if adults have to coerce children into doing it; if children are coerced, they are not in charge of scheduling the time or making decisions about the use of the time.

If we are using homework to teach responsibility, won't 10 minutes of homework work just as well as 60 minutes? If we are using homework to teach time management, don't long-range projects that require scheduled planning do a better job of that than daily assignments?

Belief #4: Lots of Homework Is a Sign of a Rigorous Curriculum

Many people equate lots of homework with a tough school, regardless of the type or length of assignments (Jackson, 2018; Lythcott-Haims, 2015). Parents will often brag, "My child goes to a really good school—he gets lots of homework." If the mind is a muscle to be trained (as was believed in the 19th century), then more work must equal more learning. If some homework is good for children, then more homework must be even better. If 10 math problems for homework is good, then 40 problems must be better. This belief, more than any other, is responsible for the piling on of hours of homework in many schools today, and it is especially entrenched in high-achieving high schools in wealthy communities.

"Heavy workload = rigor" is a false equivalency. We all know that those assignments could be busywork of no educational value (Jackson, 2018). More homework gives the *appearance* of increased rigor, and difficulty is often equated with the *amount* of work assigned, not necessarily with its level of complexity or challenge (Kohn, 2006; Williamson & Johnston, 1999). If it were only that simple. More time does not necessarily equal more learning. The "more is always better" argument ignores the quality of work and the level of learning required. Rigor is challenge—but it is not necessarily the same challenge for each student. Given the diverse nature of students, challenging learning experiences will vary for different students.

Belief #5: Good Teachers Give Homework; Good Students Do Their Homework

Probably the most disturbing belief is that homework is inherently good, regardless of the type or length of assignment. Homework advocates have believed it for years, never questioning whether it's true. This certainty is born from the assumptions that homework teaches responsibility and discipline and that "lots of homework" equals "rigor." If *good teachers give homework,* it naturally follows that teachers who don't give homework are too easy. This mindset is so ingrained that teachers apologize to other teachers for not giving homework! Yet we know that some very good teachers don't give a lot of homework or any at all. Instead of being apologetic, teachers who don't give homework should simply explain that they do such a good job of teaching that homework is not necessary.

The danger in believing that *good students do their homework* is the moral judgment that tends to accompany this belief. To children who dutifully complete homework, we often attribute the virtues of being compliant and hardworking. To children who don't complete homework, we often attribute the vices of laziness and noncompliance. But is a lack of virtue the reason many children don't do homework? Therein lies the problem. Students without supportive parents (or with single parents overburdened trying to make ends meet), with parents who don't speak English, or with inadequate home environments for completing homework are less likely to complete homework (Vatterott, 2007). Are these less advantaged students *bad?* Of course not.

Three Philosophies Underlying the Homework Culture

The five beliefs discussed in the preceding section form a dogmatic homework culture. The foundations of that culture are a trinity of very old philosophies: our moralistic views of human nature, the Puritan work ethic that is embedded in our culture, and behaviorist practices that still reside in our schools. These three philosophies are so entwined with the five beliefs that it's hard to tell where one idea ends and another begins. An exploration of these philosophies will illuminate the dogma that underlies homework culture.

Moralistic Views: Who We Believe Students Are

Historically, one mission of school has been to instill moral values. Unfortunately, much of traditional schooling operates on the theory that children are basically lazy and irresponsible, that they can't be trusted, that they have to be coerced into learning, and that they must be controlled and taught to be compliant. Therefore, it follows that it is necessary to use homework to teach responsibility.

If students have a natural tendency to do evil, then they cannot be trusted to use time wisely. Idle hands are the devil's workshop, and therefore children should not be idle. This philosophy assumes not only that children don't want to learn but also that learning is inherently distasteful. In other words, we don't *trust* students to be in charge of their own learning; instead, we believe that we must tightly control the task and method.

The Puritan Work Ethic: Who We Want Students to Be

No one would dispute that we want to encourage students to work hard. After all, hard work built America, right? The Puritans believed hard work was an honor to God that would lead to a prosperous reward. That work ethic brings to mind the stereotypical stern schoolmarm, rapping a ruler against the desk and saying "Get busy!" The tenets of the Puritan work ethic most evident in homework culture are the following:

- Hard work is good for you regardless of the pointlessness of the task.

- Hard works builds character.
- Hard work is painful; suffering is virtuous.

Here we see the origin of Belief #4, that more work equals rigor, and Belief #5, that "good" students do their homework and "good" teachers make students work hard. Unfortunately, when it comes to learning, the bleaker side of the Puritan work ethic has also taken hold. Kohn (2004) called it "the cult of rigor and the loss of joy": "If children seem to be happy in school, then not much of value could be going on there" (p. 36). And Raebeck (1992) noted that "there is a prevalent myth that if a teaching/learning experience is too enjoyable it is somehow academically suspect. If it is 'rigorous,' or better yet painful, then it must have merit" (p. 13).

The work ethic is obvious in views that homework is a way to train students how to work—that homework trains students how to study, how to work diligently and persistently, and how to delay gratification:

> As students get older, they will be called upon to delay gratification perhaps more than they would wish to. This is part of the learning process, and it is to be expected. Indeed, all manner of adult work demands persistence in the face of boredom. (Collins & Bempechat, 2017, p. 44)

Along similar lines, homework is viewed as practice for being a worker:

> Homework is *work,* not play. . . . It is assigned by a teacher for students to complete on the teacher's schedule, with the teacher's requirements in mind. So it helps to have the right attitude. Homework means business, and the student should expect to buckle down. As in the workplace, careless efforts and a laissez-faire attitude are likely to make the wrong impression . . . homework is, in part, an exchange of performance for grades. (Corno & Xu, 2004, p. 228)

The premise of Corno and Xu's article is that "homework is the quintessential job of childhood"—as though children need a job. Which raises a question: Is our job as educators to produce learners or workers?

Behaviorism: How We Think We Can Control Students

No philosophy is more firmly rooted in education than behaviorism. The idea that behavior can be controlled by rewards and punishment is so embedded in the day-to-day practices of school, one rarely even notices it (Kohn, 1999). Discipline, grades, attendance policies, honor rolls, and even the way teachers use praise and disapproval—all reflect this philosophy that behavior can be controlled by external stimuli. So it's no surprise that teachers believe rewards and punishments are the way to *make* students do homework. When punishments don't work, teachers often increase the punishment, as if more of the same will accomplish the goal.

If we believe that good students do their homework and lazy students don't, then it becomes morally defensible to give failing grades for incomplete homework, thereby punishing the vice of laziness and rewarding the virtue of hard work. Behaviorism is most evident in the use of late policies and zeros for uncompleted homework (more about that in Chapter 4).

Homework culture is so firmly entrenched in these moralistic, puritanistic, and behavioristic philosophies that traditional homework practices may be accepted without question by both teachers and parents, as if a sort of brainwashing has occurred. To use a 1970s metaphor, "if you drank the Kool-Aid," you may not realize how the cult(ure) affects your attitudes about homework.

Forces Driving the Current
Pro-Homework/Anti-Homework Debate

Homework beliefs and their historical influences affect the debate today in insidious ways. Contemporary arguments are strongly reminiscent of the earlier arguments for and against homework, yet something is different. This time around we face new and unique challenges.

The Common Core

Education's increasing focus on college and career readiness and the adoption of the Common Core State Standards by many states have upped the game. The Common Core standards require much more of students in terms of higher-level skills, including the ability to analyze, synthesize, and apply knowledge (National Governors Association Center for Best Practices [NGA Center] & Council of Chief State School Officers [CCSSO], 2010). Even states that chose not to adopt the Common Core have revised their state standards to raise the bar in a similar fashion (U.S. Department of Education, n.d.).

Although the Every Student Succeeds Act (ESSA), passed in 2015, relaxed No Child Left Behind's requirements for proficiency and removed many sanctions and penalties, standardized testing is still required, and it is unlikely that accountability will ease up. In fact, most states now include accountability for student test scores in their teacher evaluation systems. Teachers are expected to demonstrate students' academic growth and proficiency via some form of standardized testing (Porter, 2015).

As a result, the pressure to meet standards has not abated, and homework continues to be seen as a tool for meeting those standards. The repercussions of this continued pressure are visible even at the kindergarten and 1st grade levels. A University of Virginia study (Bassok, Latham, & Rorem, 2016) titled *Is Kindergarten the New First Grade?* compared kindergarten and 1st grade classrooms between 1998 and 2010 and found that kindergarten today has become more like the 1st grade of the late 1990s: the focus on academics has increased, while art, music, and playtime have decreased, and most teachers now believe students should learn to read in kindergarten.

Many parents complain that homework is now routinely assigned in kindergarten and 1st grade. According to one study, kindergartners average 25 minutes of homework a night (Pressman et al., 2015). YouTube hosts a now-famous 911 call from a 4-year-old preschooler who needed help with his "takeaway" math homework.

Media and Technology

As Thomas Friedman famously said, "The world is flat." Media and technology have broadened the homework debate to be more inclusive than in the past; more people are participating in the conversation. The Internet has given the public more information, served as a forum for many pro-homework and anti-homework blogs, and given us a window into similar debates in other countries. Today the homework debate is played out on social media and through parenting websites, as well as on radio and television and in the print media. Online parenting groups, discussion forums, and websites such as www.stophomework. com have united parents and given them strategies for protesting homework policies in their children's schools. Technology has reduced parents' isolation, enabling them to vent their once-private homework struggles publicly with the click of a mouse.

Just as the *Ladies' Home Journal* writings sparked a movement 100 years ago, during the last two decades the media has become a friend of homework reform. Since the release of Cooper's 1998 and 2006 comprehensive studies, major news magazines and talk shows have conducted a national dialogue about homework and brought increased attention to the homework reform movement. With a seemingly endless supply of television talk shows, quasi-news shows (such as *Dateline*), and round-the-clock cable news coverage, issues affecting families—including homework—have received more coverage in recent years. In addition, the availability of online media allows us to access that homework story on *Today* or that homework article in the *New York Times* whenever and wherever we want. The Internet has enabled parents to become consumers of research not only on homework but also on childhood stress, sleep, anxiety, and depression.

Media and technology have helped keep the homework debate alive as well as foster the growth of the anti-homework movement during the last few years. Given the self-feeding nature of the media, it takes only one story to reignite the debate. In the fall of 2016, a Facebook post by a Texas elementary teacher sharing her no-homework policy flooded social media and news media alike and stoked the flames of the anti-homework fire (see Figure 1.1). When parents in Spain had their children stage a "homework strike," refusing to do weekend homework, it was the strike heard around the world. Whatever the story about homework, it will show up on all the major TV networks, on CNN, on Twitter and Facebook, and in the *New York Times* and the *Washington Post*—especially at the start of the school year.

But the media industry has also been an enemy of the homework reform movement. Every year, around back-to-school time, we are buried with books, magazine articles, and television segments that reinforce a blind acceptance of homework as a good thing, endorsing the importance of homework and offering parents the same stale tips for getting children to do homework "without tears." Throughout the school year, stories appear frequently about how to get your son or daughter into the Ivy League, how to ace the SATs, or how to help your child write a killer college essay.

FIGURE 1.1
Mrs. Young's Facebook Post

"New Homework Policy"

Dear Parents:

After much research this summer, I am trying something new. Homework will only consist of work that your student did not finish during the school day. There will be no formally assigned homework this year.

Research has been unable to prove that homework improves student performance. Rather, I ask that you spend your evening doing things that are proven to correlate with student success. Eat dinner as a family, read together, play outside, and get your child to bed early.

Thanks,
Mrs. Brandy Young

Source: Printed with permission from Brandy Young.

The Mass Hysteria of "Achievement Culture"

To make matters worse, a mass hysteria has arisen among parents—especially high-income parents—about their children's ability to compete and to be successful. This "achievement culture" has become ingrained in wealthy communities throughout the United States. The American Academy of Pediatrics first labeled the trend "the professionalization of parenthood" in 2007:

> Parents receive messages from a variety of sources stating that good parents actively build every skill and aptitude their child might need from the earliest ages. . . . They hear other parents in the neighborhood talk about their overburdened schedules and recognize it is the culture and even expectation of parents. (Ginsburg, 2007, p. 185)

This mass hysteria is driven by anxiety (Abeles, 2015; Lahey, 2015; Lythcott-Haims, 2015): *It's a dog-eat-dog world, and the competition is tough. If you're not careful, you won't survive. It's a high-stakes game, and your child's future is on the line.* For many parents, the mantra has become "do whatever it takes" to get their child accepted at the best college—all of this with a tacit acceptance of the premise that admission into Harvard equals a high-paying career, which equals happiness. As one high school student put it,

> People don't go to school to learn. They go to get good grades, which brings them to college, which brings them the high-paying job, which brings them happiness, so they think. (Pope, 2001, p. 4)

And as the superintendent in one wealthy district sardonically stated, "Our parents believe there are three career paths for their children: doctor, lawyer, and unsuccessful."

There seems to be little discussion that, in fact, this could be a faulty hypothesis. Only recently have some experts advised parents to question whether the Ivy League is right for *their* child. Three faulty assumptions actually feed this trend: (1) the Ivy League is the only route to success; (2) advanced placement (AP) classes are essential to get there; and (3) excessive homework is an inevitable part of AP or honors classes.

AP Haley

Talking with other parents at a neighborhood get-together, Haley's mom is worried. Even though Haley is a good student—taking three AP classes, active in cheerleading and other activities—her mom is worried that she is not in the top 10 percent of her class. "She's only in the top 15 percent—she can't get into the University of Texas unless she's in the top 10 percent." Her mom wishes kids today weren't so competitive and claims her daughter *wants* to take three AP classes. She claims *she's* not pushing her daughter and doesn't even realize how clearly her anxiety about the future is communicated and how readily her daughter picks it up. Mom goes on to remind the others, "Look at the jobs John's kids got when they graduated from Peabody and Georgetown—all the money they are making!"

The stress is cultural—absorbed by parents and then fed to their children, creating a hypercompetitive attitude for both:

> Parents receive the message that if their children are not well prepared, well balanced, and high achieving, they will not get a desired spot in higher education. Even parents who wish to take a lower-key approach to child rearing fear slowing down when they perceive everyone else is on the fast track. (Ginsburg, 2007, p. 185)

This trend has led many parents to have a somewhat contradictory attitude toward homework. They complain about the stress homework brings to children, the battles over the dinner table, and the disruption to family life, yet at the same time they are worried about their child's ability to compete for entry into the best colleges. Although it has never been proven by research, parents assume an automatic relationship between homework and future success. They have bought into the cult of beliefs about homework and accepted a connection between hours of homework and acceptance to an elite college. Maria, a mother whose son attends a competitive college prep high school, has tears in her eyes as she describes her son going to bed at 5:00 in the evening, exhausted from his workload. But like many other parents, she is resigned to the fact that if it takes hours of homework to guarantee her son's admission to college, so be it. She and her son are victims of the "extreme expectations of an achievement culture gone crazy" (Abeles, 2015, p. 23).

One result of the mass hysteria has been a virtual explosion of the tutoring industry, now a $7 billion business in the United States alone (Boorstin, 2014). Some parents use tutoring to give their college-bound children a leg up. But more often, for parents who can afford it, the answer to the stressful and time-consuming job of supervising homework has been to "subcontract" the job to a tutor or, for the very wealthy, a "homework therapist" who will provide both academic help and emotional support to soothe student anxiety—at rates ranging from \$200 to \$600 a session (Spencer, 2018).

One of the potential negative effects of the tutoring craze has been the possibility that mass tutoring may "raise the bar" for homework assignments. After all, if most students are getting adult help with homework, it gives teachers the misperception that the students know more than they really do. It makes it appear that students are ready for more challenging assignments.

The candy factory episode of the classic *I Love Lucy* sitcom comes to mind. Lucy and Ethel are hired to work on an assembly line wrapping chocolates that pass by them on a conveyor belt. Struggling to keep up with the pace, they begin taking chocolates off the conveyor belt and stuffing them into their mouths and their hats. When the supervisor comes to check on their progress, they appear to be keeping up, so she yells to the back, "Speed it up!" Mass tutoring has the same potential to affect the difficulty of homework assignments in wealthy communities, thereby widening the gap between high-income students and disadvantaged students whose families can't afford tutors. (The gap between wealthy and disadvantaged students is discussed further in Chapter 2.)

The Balance Movement

While some parents are mired in the mass hysteria, a backlash is occurring among other parents who have become disenchanted with the hypercompetitiveness of the achievement culture. Fueled by access to research and driven by the emotional and personal experiences of their children, these parents are realizing that the push for the Ivy League has gotten out of hand and that college may not be a guaranteed ticket to success (or worth the crippling debt). The achievement culture they have bought into for so long suddenly feels wrong. They are reaching out through social media and discovering they aren't alone. They have come to realize the "cult" for the folly it is.

These parents are backing up and slowing down, seeking a balance in their children's lives. Although some are recommending that homework be abolished, many more are suggesting that excessive homework is interfering with family life and not worth the loss of a carefree childhood. The movement is less an anti-homework movement than an anti–excessive homework movement, based on the idea that children should not have longer than an eight-hour workday (Vatterott, 2003). As a reaction against the mass hysteria movement, these parents have decided they are unwilling to mortgage their son's or daughter's childhood for the nebulous promise of future success. More than 30 years ago, David Elkind warned about *The Hurried Child* (1981, 2006)—a trend to push children too hard, to overstructure their time, and to burden them with too many adult responsibilities. In 2000, *The Over-Scheduled Child: Avoiding the Hyper-Parenting Trap* (Rosenfeld & Wise) addressed similar concerns and implored parents to "ease up on the intensity" of their children's frenetic lives.

Today's balance movement echoes that advice, and it is continuing to gain support among teachers, other professionals, and the general public. The early signs of the current movement were evident around 2006, when two books landed on the *New York Times* Best Seller list: *The Overachievers: The Secret Life of Driven Kids* (Robbins, 2006) and *The Price of Privilege: How Parental Pressure and Material Advantage Are Creating a Generation of Disconnected and Unhappy Kids* (Levine, 2008). The movement was given a powerful jolt in 2009, when Vicki Abeles, a Wall Street lawyer-turned-filmmaker, released her documentary *Race to Nowhere,* which shined a spotlight on the academic stress of middle school and high school students in one affluent California community. The film was an indictment of the pressure-cooker environment that overwhelmed, overscheduled, sleep-deprived students lived in—and it named homework as a major contributor to their stress.

Race to Nowhere was distributed for free community and school screenings, and, judging by its popularity, hit a huge nerve. By 2015, more than a million people had seen the film at 7,000-plus screenings in all 50 U.S. states and more than 40 countries (Abeles, 2015). After each screening, local educators or medical professionals would facilitate audience discussions, encouraging viewers to engage with the film not as consumers but as activists and stakeholders. Those discussions proved to be an important catalyst in a nationwide grassroots movement for education reform (www.racetonowhere.com).

With the help of *Race to Nowhere*, what started as a fringe movement of a few concerned parents grew into a full-blown culture war with homework at the epicenter. Today, an increasing number of parents are demanding that schools reel in the homework load, and some parents are beginning to "just say no." One parent simply returned their child's incomplete homework with "No thank you" written on the top! (More about parent activism in Chapter 2.)

Parents who feel strongly about the need for balance worry about both the immediate and the long-term effects of excessive homework on the overall physical and psychological health of their children. The broader medical community agrees with them. As in previous periods of anti-homework sentiment, today's pediatricians are concerned about childhood issues of stress; sleep, health, and work-life balance; and loss of leisure time.

Stress. We continue to learn about the connection of stress and sleep in adults to just about everything, including physical health, psychological well-being, mental productivity, and creativity. Stress affects sleep, sleep affects stress, and exercise and downtime are needed to *de*-stress (Huffington, 2014). All these aspects of the work-life balance are interdependent, affecting one another as part of overall health for both adults and children.

Medical professionals now see the parallel between the role stress plays in adult productivity and the role it plays in student performance. As recent research with children confirms the benefits of sleep (National Sleep Foundation, 2014) and exercise (Tomporowski, Davis, Miller, & Naglieri, 2008), it also shows the detriment of stress to children's health as well as to the brain's ability to learn.

The stress levels of school-age children today are off the charts. Teens actually report higher levels of stress during the school year than do their adult counterparts. Eighty-three percent of teens named school as a major stressor (Abeles, 2015; American Psychological Association, 2014). In another study, 56 percent of high school students considered homework a primary source of stress (Galloway, Conner, & Pope, 2013).

The cover story of *Time* magazine's November 7, 2016, issue (Schrobsdorff, 2016) revealed an epidemic of anxiety and depression among adolescents, especially the most advantaged students—those who appear to have everything. Although homework is clearly not the only factor, the role it plays in such stress has come under the spotlight. In a study of more than 5,000 students in 13 high-achieving public and private middle and high schools,

> More than 70 percent of the high school students reported that they felt often or always stressed by their schoolwork, and many admitted to taking illegal stimulants to stay awake to study and complete the lengthy homework assignments each night. Very few found the homework to be useful or meaningful—which only added to their frustration with the heavy workload. (Pope, 2010, p. 4)

But it's not just teens. The alarming rise of stress is also affecting the youngest of our students. Pediatricians and counselors throughout the United States are now reporting that it is commonplace to see elementary students for stress-related symptoms, such as stomachaches and headaches, related to their anxiety over homework. One pediatrician said, "Kids are coming here with migraine headaches, ulcers. I'm talking about five-, six-, and seven-year-olds. We've never seen that before" (Abeles, 2015, p. 22).

It seems ludicrous that some adults are recommending yoga, meditation, and deep breathing for children as cures for stress. Those remedies are treating the symptom, not the problem. Children should not be this stressed about school in the first place! Still, homework is increasingly being acknowledged as a major culprit of students' stress. Stanford University now sponsors a program called Challenge Success (formerly called Stressed Out Students or S.O.S.) that works with school teams composed of the principal, students, parents, counselors, and teachers or other adults (www.challengesuccess.org) to implement school-level strategies known to improve students' mental and physical health and engagement in school. Such strategies may include homework-free holiday breaks, bans on weekend homework, flexible deadlines, study periods during the day, and shared calendars for teachers and coaches (Abeles, 2015).

Sleep, health, and work-life balance. One of the greatest concerns of pediatricians is the prevalence of sleep deprivation among school-age children. The National Sleep Foundation (2014) recommends that, for teens, nine hours of sleep is optimal, eight is borderline, and less than that is insufficient. Yet according to Eaton and colleagues (2010), the vast majority of teens get at least two hours less sleep each night than they should. As with stress, students' sleep patterns often mirror those of adults.

Only recently has research exposed the extent to which both children and adults are sleep-deprived and documented this serious issue's effects on health, mood, and intellectual functioning (Abeles, 2015). In one study, groups of 4th graders and 6th graders went to bed one hour earlier or stayed up one hour later for three nights. When their performance was tested, the short answer was "that a slightly sleepy sixth-grader will perform in class like a mere fourth-grader" (Sadeh, in Abeles, 2015, p. 25). Although sleep is influenced by many factors, such as the use of technology, caffeine, and stress, homework still makes the list as a prominent sleep thief.

Many children also sacrifice exercise and fresh air to toil over hours of homework. Recent alarming news about the level of childhood obesity and the connection between sleep deprivation and obesity (Dovey, 2018) makes a strong case for reducing homework to allow for more exercise and sleep. The now-common axioms "Sitting is the new smoking" and "Exercise is the new medicine" are sage advice for both children and adults. One child advocacy expert (Louv, 2005, 2009–2010) has actually compiled research showing that direct exposure to nature is essential for healthy physical, emotional, and spiritual development. He warns that today's overworked and overscheduled children can suffer from what he calls *nature deficit disorder*, resulting in obesity, depression, and attention deficit disorder.

Loss of leisure time. Parents often remark that, because of excessive homework, children are "losing their childhood" and "don't have time to be kids." They point to the need for fresh air, unstructured playtime, family time, and downtime.

Research on the "power of play" shows that play not only enhances social and emotional development but also has a positive effect on academic performance (Elkind, 2007). An American Academy of Pediatrics report (Milteer & Ginsburg, 2012) echoed the importance of undirected playtime for children and addressed parents' tendency to overschedule and "build résumés" for children and the negative ramifications of such actions. The report also recommended that pediatricians encourage active play and discourage overuse of passive entertainment for children, such as television and computer games. Some parents have already heeded this advice. With children's ability to be plugged in and stimulated 24/7, some parents are now beginning to limit screen time and force kids to take "media fasts." Many families are demanding no weekend or holiday homework and are prioritizing togetherness through family meals and activities like game night.

Love of learning. In addition to homework's negative effects on students' overall wellness, parents are also concerned about homework's long-term effect on children's love of learning. Of all the parental complaints about homework, this is perhaps the most poignant one: the fear that children will lose the joy of learning.

In educational circles, discussion almost exclusively focuses on short-term achievement or passing the test, not on what the practice of homework can do to a child's long-term learning, attitude about learning, or attitudes about the intellectual life. But parents are worried about the potential of excessive homework to dampen their child's natural curiosity, passion, and love of learning. Their concern, as stated by Alfie Kohn, is that homework may be "the single most reliable extinguisher of the flame of curiosity" (2006, p. 17). Have we lost the idea that the essence of schooling should be to nurture curiosity and the excitement of learning new things? (Vatterott, 2017).

A child's wonder is a tonic for the overworked, stressed-out adult. Maybe parents miss that joy of learning they no longer see in their children's eyes; maybe they need that in their lives. This is what parents are most saddened by. This is the loss they grieve the most.

Summing Up

Historically, the homework debate has continued to repeat itself. But the flawed belief that homework is grounded on has yet to be adequately challenged. What complicates today's debate is the diversity of attitudes about the value of homework. The mass hysteria and balance movements illustrate the breadth of those attitudes. As a country, the United States is so diverse economically, culturally, and in parenting styles, it is not surprising that not all would agree on a practice that bridges both school and family life. This diversity of attitudes requires not only a critical examination of homework practices but also a rethinking of the school-family relationship. This changing dynamic between parents and schools is discussed in Chapter 2.

Homework in the Context of the New Family

Homework occurs within the context of both school and family, but the traditional practices of homework may be out of sync with the needs of today's families. The incredible diversity among families presents many challenges to the successful implementation of homework. Families are more economically and culturally diverse than in the past, and family composition is more varied than ever before, with divorced parents and blended families increasingly common, and with more grandparents than ever raising their grandchildren. Today's families exhibit a variety of parenting styles and values, some of which may be mismatched with the values of teachers and schools.

In previous generations, mainstream America seemed to agree about issues like honesty, respect for authority, and child rearing. Children received similar messages about right and wrong from their school, place of worship, home, and neighborhood. If it takes a village to raise a child, in previous generations the village *was* raising the child. Adults seemed to agree about what was best for children. In some communities today, those shared values still exist, but in others that consistency of message is sorely lacking (Taffel, 2001).

The 1960s "do your own thing" generation marked the beginning of a diversity of family and societal values that continues to widen. As our society grows more diverse, students and parents may no longer receive consistent messages from their family, religion, community, and school. Parents value their individuality and freedom to set their own standards about child rearing. A broad diversity of opinions exists about such things as whether children should attend religious services, be paid for chores, or have curfews. On almost any given parenting topic, it is difficult for a group of parents to reach consensus. Regardless of how similar parents in a school appear to be, it is unlikely that all will have the same opinions about parenting or how homework should be handled.

Economic diversity, cultural diversity, and different parenting styles and family values converge to have an effect on homework, creating differing views of the parent-school relationship and differing attitudes about homework. A diversity in family values makes it even more likely that those values will clash with the values of individual teachers. Can we teach without judging the values of our students' families? It is important for educators to understand the complexity of today's families and to respect individual family values when implementing homework as an instructional practice.

Diversity of Parenting Styles

The evolution of democracy, in the United States and around the world, has profoundly affected families. Children, once viewed as powerless, are gaining legal rights and protections once reserved only for adults (Vatterott, 2007). This shift has influenced power relationships within families; traditional power relationships have given way to more democratic, egalitarian relationships between parents and children.

The current generation of children is the most democratically raised in U.S. history—protected by law against abuse and neglect and often allowed to make decisions at an early age about what they eat and wear, and what toys their parents buy. As U.S.

culture has become more democratic, a diversity of power relationships has emerged among families. A significant change in parenting style that affects homework has been the trend away from authoritative parenting and toward more democratic families. One might call it "the death of the dictatorship" in parenting.

Parenting a dictatorship? To understand the analogy, one need only listen to adults who grew up in the 1950s talk about their childhood. Many of them will remark that "children didn't have rights" in those days. Children did what they were told, ate whatever food was put in front of them, and wore the clothes their parents picked out for them. They did their homework because they were told to. The parent-child relationship was definitely top-down, and children were relatively powerless. This traditional power structure still exists in some families and in some cultures today, but it is not as prevalent as it once was. When teachers say, "Why can't the parents just *make* their children do their homework?" they may be visualizing a dictatorial style of parenting that no longer exists in those families.

In many families, parental control of children has become less absolute. Many parents today have vowed not to be the dictators their parents were. They have allowed their children to have input into decisions, and they have often negotiated compromises with their children. More traditional parents (and more traditional teachers) will claim *that* is the problem with homework—that children have been given the impression that everything is negotiable and that parents have allowed children to be in charge. In a few families, parents may have lost a clear sense of their authority, and children may have learned how to be in control. But in most families, parents are firmly in charge even though children have input into decisions.

How does parenting style affect homework? Rather than controlling all aspects of their child's life, parents who are not dictators are much more likely to choose their battles. Unfortunately, homework has become a big battle and a source of stress in many families. One study (Pressman et al., 2015) found that parental stress levels were higher when parents lacked confidence in their ability to help, when English was not their first language, and when their child disliked homework. No surprise here. Many parents are tired of the tension, the teary battles at the kitchen table, and the nagging they have to do to get the homework completed. They do not want to be the teacher's enforcer or, as some parents call it, the "homework cop." Frustrated by their inability to force their children to do boring tasks or to continue to work when they are tired, many parents have decided that homework is not a battle they want to fight.

When asked what she thought about problems with homework, one family counselor said, "The problem with homework is that parents are wimps" (meaning that they are no longer dictators). Maybe parents are not wimps; maybe they are smarter than we give them credit for. Maybe they realize the lack of value of some homework tasks, and maybe they know their children well enough to know when they need downtime.

Diversity of Beliefs About the Place of Academic Work in Life

Parents also differ in their beliefs about the place of academic work in a balanced life. Parents of all socioeconomic levels have a variety of opinions about the importance of homework in their child's daily life and what the balance should be between homework and other activities. Again, these beliefs may not be compatible with teacher beliefs.

All Academics, All the Time

Some parents believe that homework is the avenue through which all virtue flows. To them, academic life is the priority—as Corno (1996) once said, "Homework is the job of childhood." For children in the All Academics, All the Time families, homework totally defines a child's free time. These parents believe homework is one way they can help their child get ahead and that it is the path to lifetime achievement (Kralovec & Buell, 2000; Lythcott-Haims, 2015). At a parent meeting in which school officials were discussing a new policy limiting homework, one parent asked, "Well, then, what would they do with their time?" Part of the rationale for All Academics, All the Time is the belief, discussed in Chapter 1, that intellectual activity is intrinsically more valuable than nonintellectual pursuits and that homework is better than television or video games. This attitude indicates a false sense of security that homework will somehow keep children out of trouble, away from vices like sex, alcohol, and drugs. The All Academics, All the Time mindset lacks an understanding of the value of play, leisure pursuits, and downtime in a child's physical, intellectual, and psychological development (Abeles, 2015; Elkind, 2007; Huffington, 2014).

All Academics, All the Time parents often ask for extra homework for their child and become nervous when there is no homework to fill weekends and vacations. They seem to assume that as long as their kids have homework to do every night—never mind what it is—then learning must be taking place. Educational quality is assumed to be synonymous with rigor, and rigor, in turn, is thought to be reflected by the quantity and difficulty of assignments (Abeles, 2015; Kohn, 2006). If teachers have no suggestions for enrichment activities, these parents will often create homework for their children, making them study or review previous work.

Balancing Academics and Family-Chosen Activities

Another group of parents wishes to balance homework with other outside activities they and their child have chosen. These parents often claim they want their child to be well rounded, while some are also feeding the high school résumé to enhance their child's college opportunities. Whatever the reason, many children are involved in numerous outside activities after school.

Teachers may feel entitled to counsel parents on the over-scheduling of their child, but this is a slippery slope. It is certainly within our jurisdiction to recommend that students take fewer advanced placement classes (if we feel that taking those classes is contributing to homework overload), or to be concerned if students appear exhausted or overly stressed. But we must be careful that we truly have the best interest of the child in mind, rather than just wanting to see homework completed.

Parents have the right to control their child's time outside school. Parents frequently complain about students being forced to miss activities such as scout meetings or piano lessons because of excessive homework. Religious, cultural, or family traditions must also be respected. In some communities, homework is not assigned on Wednesday evenings because so many children attend church that evening. Many parents would like their children to attend an evening religion studies class one night a week. Catholic students who attend public school may take religion classes one evening a week in preparation for First Communion or confirmation. In many cultures, Saturday or Sunday is designated as family day, when time spent with family takes priority over schoolwork. These examples offer just a few reasons to eliminate homework on weekends or during vacations.

Balancing Academics, Leisure, and Happiness

Many parents simply feel their children's lives are too busy and would like them to have more leisure time. "They just need time to play," "We just want them to be able to do nothing sometimes," "It would be nice to have time to hang out with our kids and maybe watch a television show together," parents will say. They instinctively realize that their children's lives are too hectic, that their children are not relaxed or are not getting adequate sleep. One parent of a 6th grader in a gifted program complained that her daughter had two to three hours of homework a night. "The attitude of the teacher and administration seems to be that 'if she can't do the work maybe she doesn't belong here.' We are torn between wanting the challenge of the program and concern for our daughter's overall well-being."

Parents are also concerned about the stress that homework brings to children's daily routine. Some young children are exhausted after school and struggle to complete any homework at all. These are children who fairly recently were still taking naps in the afternoon (Kohn, 2006). Empathic parents and authors Bennett and Kalish (2006) provide a metaphor:

> For many kids, homework is like having to do their taxes *every night.* How would we feel if we came home to hours of work from five different bosses? At least some of us would quit or enter therapy—which is where some of our children now find themselves. (p. 22)

Divorced parents and parents with unusual work schedules also have concerns. Many noncustodial divorced parents complain that they see their child only a few hours a week, and they don't want to spend that time fighting over homework. Parents who work evenings or do shift work may have only occasional blocks of time to spend with their child, and when they do, they want it to be relaxed, enjoyable time. Is it any wonder that for these families quality time takes precedence over homework?

The Priority of Family Responsibilities and Paid Work

For some children, especially those from low-income families, time after school is a precious resource for a family stretched thin. Those children's families may need them to babysit younger siblings, cook meals, do laundry, or clean. For families who own businesses or farms, children are a valuable part of the workforce. (How often do you see school-age children helping out in small family-owned restaurants?) In these situations, homework could actually be taking money out of the family's pocket.

Homework Clashes with Family Needs

Administrators at one Wisconsin middle school realized that many students were not completing homework and, as a result, failing classes. In the fall, a mandatory after-school program was established Mondays through Thursdays that required students to stay after school to make up missing homework assignments. A letter was sent home to parents at the beginning of the year explaining the purpose of the program and assuring them that after-school transportation would be provided. Teachers and administrators believe the program is working well, preventing many students from failing, and it has been well received overall. However, one parent complained that the program has cost her $210 month for babysitting this month because her son has been staying after school. This frustrated the administrator, who feels gratified that the boy is no longer failing. But to that parent, the financial priority is more critical than the incomplete homework.

unintended consequence!

As this vignette shows, family values sometimes conflict with the values of the school. Even when the financial need is not dire, many families believe strongly in the value of paid work. As soon as their children are old enough to work, they expect them to start building an employment record. This is viewed as a legitimate method of teaching responsibility and money management, as well as preparation for a future life in the workforce. Whether students actually *need* to work is irrelevant to us as educators. It is the family value driving the decision that must be respected.

What does all this mean for homework? The diversity of family values and family priorities and individual differences in students render a one-size-fits-all homework plan virtually useless. Some parents will want more homework; some will want less. Some students will succeed with very full schedules, whereas others will thrive only when given adequate downtime to de-stress. This diversity of daily life after school also speaks volumes to the antiquated practice of assigning homework at 3:00 p.m. on Tuesday and expecting it back at 8:00 a.m. on Wednesday. Teachers need to accept that on certain evenings it will be impossible for some students to complete homework.

Teachers must be careful not to focus so intensely on learning that they lose sight of the importance of family life. Teachers will need to remain flexible about family priorities and also learn more about their individual students' schedules outside school. Many teachers have replaced daily homework with monthly or weekly lists, or a course syllabus showing all homework assignments for the semester. This approach allows more flexibility for the students and enables them to plan ahead for conflicts.

Diversity of Parental Involvement in Homework

Parents' involvement in the homework process can run the gamut from no involvement at all to regularly completing their children's homework for them. That involvement may vary depending on the age of the student, the ability level of the student, the educational level of the parent, and the time the parent has available.

At one end of the continuum are parents who do not get involved at all with their child's homework. They don't ask if their child has homework, nor do they check to see if it is completed. They may care about their child's education but simply do not have the time, energy, or opportunity to be involved. Many parents are uninvolved because they have made a conscious decision to take a hands-off approach. Many have stopped being involved with homework because they are tired of the battle. They don't *want* the job, and they don't think it should *be* their job. As one parent said, "Teachers want us to do their job. Parents should not be expected to morph into tutors by night." Those parents feel it is the teacher's job to work with the student to ensure that homework is completed. Uninvolved parents will often say, "If it's supposed to help the child be responsible, why is it *my* job?" Many parents of high school students, in an effort to help their children be more independent, have stopped supervising homework. How do uninvolved parents feel about their lack of involvement? Some are quite comfortable, some are resentful that they are *expected* to be involved, and some feel guilty that they are being judged as bad parents.

On the other end of the continuum are the overinvolved parents, nicknamed "helicopter parents" (see further discussion on pp. 49–51) because of their tendency to hover over their child's education, scrutinizing every move of the teacher and the student (Lahey, 2015; Lythcott-Haims, 2015). These are the parents who often micromanage homework and won't hesitate to do homework for the child to ensure a good grade. Why do these parents micromanage? There could be several reasons: being fearful of the child's failing, overprotecting the child from unpleasantness, or saving the child from pain by not allowing the child to make mistakes. Punitive grading practices inadvertently encourage this overinvolvement from parents.

Many of these parental behaviors are self-imposed—you will often hear parents say, "I need to make sure the homework is right," "I feel I must be involved," "If I don't help them, they will fail," and "I know I shouldn't do the work for them, but I just can't help myself." Do these statements sound a little obsessive-compulsive? As any psychologist will tell you, this kind of behavior is often driven by the desire to reduce anxiety—in this case, parental anxiety spurred on by the mass hysteria about their children's future that was discussed in Chapter 1.

Unfortunately, this classic enabling behavior often does more harm than good. By micromanaging and taking responsibility for homework, these parents risk disabling their children's self-reliance and may even rob the children of their own sense of accomplishment. Parents also send a message to their children that they don't trust them to do the work. The children quickly learn that if they act helpless, their parents will do the job for them. This may seem like protective and compassionate behavior on the part of parents, but it eventually backfires when children get to middle school and high school.

Some parents will say that it's necessary to be so involved, that homework has changed and become more complex (Bennett & Kalish, 2006; Lythcott-Haims, 2015). Is homework today really so different? If homework is so complex that students cannot complete it on their own, that is a problem that should be addressed with the teacher, not by doing the work for the child. But many parents seem unwilling or unable to discuss homework with teachers, afraid to question if the amount or difficulty of homework assignments is right for their child. They accept that this homework must be what needs to be done.

Economic Diversity Issues: The "Haves" and the "Have-Nots"

Economic diversity of families holds perhaps the greatest challenge as schools struggle to implement fair and equitable homework policies. During the last 30 years, increasing economic diversity has created an ever-widening chasm between the rich and the poor (Reardon, 2013). Since 1980, the share of income going to the top 1 percent has more than doubled (Newman, 2017), and the middle class has shrunk (Fry & Kochhar, 2016). In other words, the rich are getting richer and the poor are getting poorer, and the number of children living in poverty continues to rise.

For the first time in recent history, the majority of children attending our K–12 public schools come from low-income families. By the latest reliable data (Suitts, 2016), 52 percent of students in U.S. public schools are eligible to receive free or reduced-price lunch. Today, low-income students are the majority in 21 states; in 19 other states, they constitute between 40 and 49 percent of public school enrollment (Suitts, 2016).

This economic and social bifurcation of wealth and poverty has major implications for education in general and homework in particular. Socioeconomic status (SES) separates the haves from the have-nots in several concrete ways, all of which can affect learning. The works of Richard Rothstein (2004, 2010) and Eric Jensen (2013) document important gaps between low-SES home environments and higher-SES home environments. First, there is a *reading gap*—low-SES students may not have books in the home, are less likely to be read to in the home, and are less likely to see their parents reading for pleasure or reading to solve problems (Rothstein, 2004). Second, there is a *conversation gap*:

> Children from low-income families hear, on average, 13 million words by age 4. In middle-class families, children hear about 26 million words during that same time period. In upper-income families, they hear a staggering 46 million words by age 4—three times as many as their lower-income counterparts. . . . This language difference is not subtle; it's a mind-boggling jaw-dropping cognitive chasm. (Jensen, 2013, p. 25)

Third, there is a *health and housing gap*—students from low-income households, in general, are in poorer health than students from middle- or upper-income households. As a result of poorer prenatal conditions, unhealthy environments, and lack of medical care, students from low-SES families are more likely to have vision problems, dental problems, and asthma. Because they often lack health insurance, they are more likely to miss school for minor health problems that go untreated, such as ear infections. All these factors put these children at a disadvantage even before they enter school (Jensen, 2013; Rothstein, 2010).

In 2014, FCC Commissioner Jessica Rosenworcel coined the term *homework gap* to describe another disadvantage for children living in poverty. Noting that roughly 7 in 10 teachers assign homework that requires access to broadband Internet but that almost one in three households do not subscribe to these services, Rosenworcel called the homework gap "the cruelest part of the digital divide." But the homework gap goes beyond Internet access: it is often indicative of broader gaps between social classes' access to quality schools, home resources, and other educational assistance.

For children with special needs, class differences are especially important because they often influence the amount and quality of learning assistance these children receive. Consider the following examples of Andre and Tyler, two 3rd grade boys with learning disabilities.

Same Need, Different Outcome

Andre is from a lower-income family. His parents are both high school dropouts and understand little about the concept of learning disabilities. They know Andre has always struggled in school, but they have trouble taking time off from their jobs to talk to the teacher. They feel uncomfortable talking to people at the school and do not know it is possible for Andre to be tested for a learning disability or to receive special help. They cannot afford to send Andre to a tutor. Andre lags far behind the other 3rd graders in reading and math.

Tyler also has a learning disability, but his story is much different. His parents are wealthy and highly educated. Before kindergarten, they participated in a school-sponsored parenting program, which taught them how to enhance Tyler's cognitive development. When he performed poorly on the kindergarten screening, they paid to have a comprehensive assessment done through a child development center at a local hospital. Tyler's parents had him tested by the school in kindergarten, advocated for special placement with the best teachers, and closely monitored his progress. Tyler and his parents regularly see a family counselor, and Tyler gets weekly help from a tutor. As a result, in the 3rd grade Tyler is close to grade level in reading and math.

As these stories illustrate, class differences can easily create disadvantages at school for children from low-income families. Unfortunately, homework has the potential to exacerbate class differences and widen the achievement gap—and not just in the United States. A study by the Organisation for Economic Co-operation and Development (2015) of students from 38 different countries showed that students from higher social classes did more homework than students from lower social classes.

The more affluent students also performed better on the PISA (Programme for International Student Assessment) standardized test, which led some to conclude that homework *caused* that difference in test scores, although it is just as possible that differences in school quality were at play.

In the worst-case scenario, homework helps the privileged succeed academically and causes the less privileged to fail academically. When Kralovec and Buell (2000) asked former high school dropouts in Maine which factors contributed to their decision to drop out of school, one of the top reasons given was their inability to keep up with homework. That's a powerful indictment of the effect of homework on students in poverty. Consider the lives of the following three high school students—Emma, Hannah, and Sofia—and how their families' economic situations affect their ability to complete homework.

Homework and the Socioeconomic Divide

Even when Emma has several hours of homework, she always completes it. Her parents take pride in how hard she works, convinced that rigorous homework will prepare Emma for an Ivy League education. Emma's parents both have advanced degrees, and they often have intellectual discussions with Emma about the subjects she is studying. They have an extensive home library, Internet access, and plenty of money to hire tutors and purchase materials for homework projects. Emma has her own computer. In her pursuit of the perfect grade point average, Emma has learned how to cut corners and even cheat when necessary, and how to do without sleep and a social life in order to be a successful student.

Hannah usually does her homework. Although her parents are not highly educated, they value education, and it is important to them that Hannah do well in school. Both her parents work long hours, and their free time is often consumed with household chores. Though their schedules seem overwhelming, Hannah's parents usually find time to monitor her homework but often do not understand the content. Sometimes they drive her to the store for homework materials. The family has one computer that several people must share. Hannah's parents usually check to make sure Hannah has done her homework.

Sofia often does not do her homework. She comes home immediately after school three days a week to care for her younger siblings so her single mother can go to work. The other two days, Sofia
works part-time after school to supplement her mother's paycheck.
Even when she has time, circumstances make it difficult for her to
complete homework. There is no quiet place in the house to study,
and there is no computer. Sofia's mother has only a 6th grade education and does not speak English, so it is hard for her to help Sofia
with homework. The family budget has no money for materials for
homework projects. Even if money were available, the family has no
car for the trip to the store. It is not safe to walk to the public library.

Obviously, these scenarios do not represent all students—
not all high-SES students are like Tyler and Emma, and not all
low-SES students are like Andre and Sofia. There is no one typical
situation for any social class. Although differences in homework
completion exist among students regardless of social class, the
scenarios illustrate the discrepancy in the homework experience
that *can* occur across social classes. For poor families, homework may be a low priority compared to survival (Dueck, 2014).
If those parents feel that school has not benefited them in their
lives, they may see homework as a waste of time in view of the
more essential needs of preparing meals, caring for younger children, and working to provide money for the family.

As illustrated in the stories related here, students from
low-income families are likely to have more obstacles to completing homework than students from higher-income families. More
affluent parents are more likely than less affluent parents to help
with homework (Lythcott-Haims, 2015; Rothstein, 2004). When
children are unable to complete homework because of family or
economic conditions, teachers run the risk of unfairly punishing
those children for factors beyond their control. Homework is
most unfair when teachers fail to realize the limitations of the
homework environment for students from low-income families.

What if the way teachers use homework worsened the
achievement gap between rich and poor students? Would that

fact cause us to consider the use of homework more carefully? When creating homework tasks, teachers should guard against assumptions about a child's home environment. When assigning homework, the following advice should be followed:

- Do not assume the child has a quiet place to do homework.
- Do not assume the child has a parent home in the evening.
- Do not assume the child's parents speak and read English.
- Do not assume the family has money for school supplies.
- Do not assume the child has access to materials such as paper, a pencil sharpener, scissors, glue, magazines, or a calculator.
- Do not assume the child has access to a computer or the Internet.

The Changing Parent-School Relationship

As any veteran teacher will tell you, dealing with parents today is different than it was in the past. As families have changed, their relationship with the school has changed as well, which brings us to an important but delicate discussion about the parent-school relationship. This section discusses the social changes that have led to corresponding changes in the parent-school relationship, the demise of the absolute authority of the school, and the separate power structures of home and school.

Social Changes Behind the Shift

The changing parent-school relationship is actually the result of decades of social change: the evolution of a more democratic society, the rise of the "overparenting" movement, and a growing parental frustration with changes in K–12 education.

The evolution of a more democratic society. To understand where we are, we must first reflect on where we have been. In previous generations, society was more authoritarian, and people were usually respectful of that authority. Schools, representing a sanctioned societal organization, maintained the status quo with absolute authority over children. In the authority hierarchy, teachers ruled over students, and parents seldom questioned the authority of the school. Parents were a silent partner with the school, rarely entering into the decision-making process. When teachers asked for parental involvement, what they really meant was they wanted parents to help them reach the academic goals that they, as the educational experts, had deemed important.

Parents assumed the school knew best. When children were assigned homework, parents dutifully obliged schools by making sure homework was done. For the many mothers who didn't work outside the home, taking responsibility for homework was less of a hardship than it is for many working parents today. Parents were willing partners in the homework practice. Although that scenario may still exist in some schools today, in many communities the relationship looks much different.

As the culture and families became more democratic, a sense of empowerment grew among parents, a feeling that they "had the right" to have a say in their child's education. Whereas in the past, parents had trusted that the school knew best, parents began to believe *they* knew something about education too. Teachers were no longer the only educational experts in the room. Teachers began to complain that "everyone's an expert on education just because they went to school." Parents began to voice opinions about many decisions being made in the school—about discipline, schedules, vacations, dress codes, and the like.

The rise of overparenting. The second social change has been the rise of *overparenting*—also labeled *hyper-parenting* or *helicopter parenting* (Lahey, 2015; Lythcott-Haims, 2015). It is not limited to wealthy or college-educated parents, but it is certainly more prevalent among them.

The word *parent* wasn't used as a verb until a few decades ago. In fact, some experts argue that it was only in the 1990s that the idea of "parenting" became a full-fledged "thing" (Wong, 2016). By that time, at least for members of the middle class, being a parent didn't just mean serving as an authority figure and a source of sustenance and support for a child—it meant molding that child's life, flooding her with opportunity so she could have a competitive edge in the long term, and enriching her with all kinds of constructive experiences (Wong, 2016).

Whereas the democratization of our culture led parents to believe they had the *right* to have a say in their child's education, the overparenting movement caused parents to feel the *need* to be vocal about their child's education. It created a sense of advocacy and, to teachers' chagrin, even urgency—as in "Why haven't the grades for the test you gave today been posted yet?"

A recent story in the *New York Times* (Spencer, 2017) provides a telling snapshot of today's parents, speaking volumes about parent advocacy, economic inequities, and the challenges school leaders face in navigating the new parent-school relationship. The story details how P.S. 11, a preK–5th grade school in an economically diverse neighborhood in Manhattan, had decided to ban mandatory traditional homework for students up to 4th grade. Instead, the school encouraged students to read nightly and directed parents to a website offering ideas for engaging after-school activities. Given the growing anti-homework sentiment in the United States, one might assume that parents' reaction would be delight. Instead, the policy divided parents, often along class lines:

> Some privately called the plan "economically and racially insensitive," favoring families with time and money to provide their own enrichment. . . . [A] single mother with three children at the school . . . said the policy had created an unwelcome burden on her and other less affluent families that could not afford extra workbooks, or software programs to supplement the new policy. (paras. 2, 4)

This story offers some insights into parental thinking. First, it shows how deeply embedded parents' belief in the value of homework is—that homework offers an advantage and that without it, children cannot succeed academically. Second, fear of competition is alive and well. For busy lower-income parents, there was almost a paranoia about the ability of the higher-income parents to give their children an advantage. Finally, although some parents are clearly happy to invest time and money in customizing homework and choosing engaging activities for their children, other parents do not *want* that responsibility. Some parents are still more comfortable with traditional, familiar homework tasks like worksheets.

Growing parental frustration with changes in K–12 education. Parental protests about homework are symptomatic of a larger trend that has emerged since the first edition of this book was published in 2009. In the *New York Times* article just discussed, Columbia University professor Tom Hatch called the homework wars "a proxy fight about what constitutes learning" and "'a small part of a larger conversation about how kids should spend their time'" (Spencer, 2017, paras. 5, 6).

I liken it to post-traumatic stress, arising after federal mandates put standardized tests front and center and the Common Core turned curriculum on its head. Complaints about homework practices are enmeshed with debates about standardized testing, which have fueled a national "opt-out" movement. Many parents believe that both the Common Core and standardized testing have caused teachers to ramp up the amount and complexity of homework. Homework has become just one more thing about education that parents are fed up with and feel powerless to control.

What was once advocacy has morphed into activism, with the global cyber-village emboldening parents to demand what they believe is in the best interest of their child. Picture the classic movie scene from *Network*: "I'm as mad as hell, and I'm not going to take this anymore!" Parents now publicly and unapologetically take to social media, blogs, and newspaper editorials to vent their frustration. For me, a personal favorite and contender for the "You can't make this stuff up!" award is end-of-year homework-burning parties: "It's when a group of kids and parents get together, make a big fire, throw in all of their old homework from the year, and watch it burn" (Stahl, 2017, para. 3). That's a pretty vivid illustration of the new breed of parent frustration and activism.

The Demise of the Absolute Authority of the School

The days of the absolute authority of the school are over. Mirroring the death of the dictatorship in families discussed earlier, the school dictatorship is the victim of parent activism. Many parents today feel not only that school decisions *can be* challenged, but also that they *should be* challenged. Many parents no longer view themselves as partners with teachers in the job of educating their child, but more like clients of a service to be delivered. Instead of believing that they owe the school support, many parents feel that the school owes them a service. Coupled with this belief is the concept of parental freedom—that parents have the right to raise their children as they see fit.

If this picture of parental support seems bleak, it is meant to be. It is meant to shock us into a reality check. Do all parents today feel that way about school? Of course not. But it is important to understand the perspective of those parents and to realize that the disconnect between the school's view and parents' views can be a major problem. We must be self-critical as educators and acknowledge that, in many schools, our relationship with parents has never been a partnership, especially when it comes to homework. Two moms expressed it this way:

> Few parents would call what we have with our kids' schools a "partnership" when we rarely have a say about our "part" or whether we want to turn our homes into second classrooms at night. (Bennett & Kallish, 2006, p. 58)

When teachers and principals complain that parents are no longer supportive of the school and teachers, they may be living in the past—when being *supportive* parents meant doing exactly what the teacher wanted, no questions asked. Those teachers and principals have failed to realize that a fundamental paradigm shift has occurred in the power relationship between parents and schools.

The Separate Power Structures of Home and School

Schools and families have always maintained separate power structures. For the most part, schools did not tell families how to raise their children, and parents did not tell schools how to teach their students. Parents maintained power over their children in the family, and teachers maintained power over children when they were at school. The school was expected to act *in loco parentis,* in place of the parent. Parents, in that sense, relinquished control of their children during the school day, when teachers acted in their place.

Schools have extended their reach into the family power structure in only a few areas, serving as agents of the state to protect the best interest of the child. For instance, schools intervene to ensure that students attend school regularly and have had their immunizations. Schools are required by law to report abuse and neglect. Schools can prohibit sick children from attending school and can remove students who are a danger to others. But recently, when some schools began sending letters home to parents indicating their children were overweight (Watson, 2014), parents quickly protested that the school had unreasonably crossed the boundary between school and parental power structures. Increasing numbers of parents now believe homework has crossed that boundary as well (Abeles, 2015; Kohn, 2015). Homework has become a contentious battleground in the fragile relationship between parents and school. As Goldberg (2007) puts it,

> Homework is an anomaly that transverses the boundary between family and school. It is a standard created at school for behavior to take place in the home. There is no other area in a child's life where an authority outside the parent has so much influence on policies and practices at home. (p. 4)

Homework is treated as a policy, not as a suggestion, with the school having the power to exact punishment if it does not get done (Goldberg, 2012).

Renegotiating the Parent-School Relationship

If parents are graciously compliant about homework and children dutifully complete homework with no negative effects, perhaps your school has no problem. But for those parents who have concerns, it will be necessary for teachers and principals to revise their expectations and renegotiate the relationship between school and parent.

Renegotiating the relationship will require teachers to compromise, respect parents' wishes, and relax a bit. One of our biggest handicaps as educators is our own anxiety about poor student performance and the belief that homework will save poorly performing students. Forging a true partnership for homework will require some hard work and some tough thinking. The following steps are a good start.

1. Get real. Homework critics bluntly state that schools should not be dictating what children do with their evenings (Abeles, 2015; Kohn, 2015). Principals and teachers must accept that they are not totally in charge of a child's free time and that they do not have the right to demand that parents be involved with and support homework. That does not mean they must give up on homework completely—it just means they must be willing to compromise and respect the wishes of parents to control their child's time outside school.

2.   Resist the temptation to judge. As teachers, it is easy to feel powerless when we need help, can't control parents, and feel overwhelmed. If we are teaching in a school with few resources, it is particularly frustrating. That frustration makes it tempting for teachers to judge—it's easy to blame both the parents and the student when homework is not completed. One teacher who was raised in poverty complained, "I did it. I was poor, but I knew it was my responsibility to do the homework, so I did it. If I did it, they can, too." Perhaps she had supportive parents who strongly valued education, and perhaps she was blessed with drive and perseverance. Regardless of our own upbringing, this tendency to judge families from the perspective of the way *we* were raised is damaging to the parent-school relationship.

Sometimes it's easier to judge children as unmotivated or lazy than to reflect on our own teaching methods or to admit we don't have the tools, experience, or training to meet individual students' needs. But judging, blaming, and whining solve nothing. Teachers must accept the limitations of parental involvement and find ways to work with the support they have.

3.   Revise expectations of parental support. An AP-AOL poll indicated a disparity between teacher and parent views of homework help. When parents were asked, "Thinking about the amount of time you spend helping your child with homework, do you feel it is usually too much, about right, or too little?" Fifty-seven percent of parents thought they were spending about the right amount of time. However, when teachers were asked, "In general, how would you rate the amount of time most parents spend helping their children with homework?" only 8 percent of teachers answered "about the right amount of time," and 87 percent of teachers answered "not enough time" (Rebora, 2006). This discrepancy might lead one to offer the following advice to teachers: When all else fails, lower your expectations!

What are reasonable expectations? Chapters 3 and 4 discuss the specific types of tasks that are best for homework, but suffice it to say here that homework should not be used for new learning (Jackson, 2018). Parents should not be expected to teach their child a new skill. If the child has been given an assignment but has not yet acquired the skill, then the homework is inappropriate (Vatterott, 2010).

Expectations are not demands. It is important to get parents' feedback about how much they want to be involved and to respect the wishes of individual parents. Schools should not expect that all parents will be involved with homework—that is the parent's choice.

4. Suggest (do not mandate) guidelines for the parent's role in homework. Most parents are unclear about what their role in homework is supposed to be. They often get different messages from different teachers as to what and how much they are supposed to do. They need more guidance and more communication from the teacher about expectations, but they also want teachers to respect what they as parents are willing and able to do in the homework process.

Parents should be encouraged to be *less involved* with the child's actual homework task and *more involved* in communicating with the teacher—writing notes when students don't complete work, asking for adaptations, or documenting how much time the child spent on the task. Parents should be encouraged to be observers, not enforcers (Goldberg, 2012).

If the child cannot do the homework without help, parents should be directed to stop the child and write a note to the teacher. If doing homework with their child is causing stress or conflict, parents should be directed to stop helping (Goldberg, 2012). Parents should inform the school if they believe their child's homework load is excessive.

It is logical to expect parents to be somewhat more involved at the elementary level, less involved at the middle school level, and rarely involved at the high school level. During middle school, parents should be encouraged to wean their child off their homework help. Parents can be instructed to tell their children, "It's time for me to quit helping you with your homework" or "Mom's not taking algebra this year" (Lythcott-Haims, 2015; Vatterott, 2005). At the middle and high school levels, parents should back off tasks such as correcting mistakes, proofreading, and reviewing for tests. By this age, students should be self-checking and working with classmates to study or peer-edit. Homework advice for 7th and 8th grade parents should be "Don't touch it, don't pack it." At the middle and high school levels, teachers should work with students directly to make sure homework is completed and turned in. This assumes, of course, that school strategies are in place to prevent the student from failing as a result of incomplete homework (see the discussion of homework support programs in Chapter 5).

As schools attempt to define the parent's role in homework, they must realize that they can only *recommend* what parents should do. Given the new relationship between parents and schools, it would seem counterproductive for schools to *mandate* parental involvement in homework. Schools should work with their building's parent-teacher organization to come up with suggestions that clarify the parent's role in the homework process.

When designing homework guidelines for parents, wording is important. The phrases *parent guidelines* or *parent options* suggest a voluntary process, that parents have choices in what they will or will not do with regard to homework. *Parent expectations,* however, indicates that teachers *expect* parents to do certain things, meaning that if parents *don't* do those things, they—or their children—may be judged poorly. An example of suggested guidelines for the parent's role in homework is shown in Figure 2.1.

FIGURE 2.1
Suggested Guidelines for Parental Involvement in Homework

Parents are encouraged to . . .
Ask their child about what the child is studying in school.
Ask their child to show them any homework assignments.
Assist their child in organizing homework materials.
Help their child formulate a plan for completing homework.
Provide an appropriate space for their child to do homework.

Parents may, if they wish . . .
Help their child interpret assignment directions.
Proofread their child's work, pointing out errors.
Read aloud required reading to their child.
Give practice quizzes to their child to help prepare for tests.
Help their child brainstorm ideas for papers or projects.
Praise their child for completing homework.

Parents should not . . .
Attempt to teach their child concepts or skills the child is unfamiliar with.
Complete assignments for their child.
Allow their child to sacrifice sleep to complete homework.

---

5. Establish formal methods of parent-teacher communication. A true partnership involves two-way communication that can be initiated by either party. Yet often school communication is one-way, with school officials telling parents what they or their children should be doing (Ferlazzo, 2011). Parents need guidance and specific tools to help them communicate with teachers about homework. When necessary, these tools should be made available in multiple languages (Horsley & Walker, 2013).

A home schedule card (shown in Figure 2.2) allows parents or students to list their outside commitments. This can provide valuable information to teachers as they adapt assignments and deadlines to meet individual needs. A short parent survey such as the one shown in Figure 2.3 can help teachers understand parents' views about homework and their preferred level of involvement. (A longer version of the parent survey, along with teacher and student surveys, appears in the appendix.)

FIGURE 2.2
Home Schedule Card for Parents

Child's name_____

Grade level_____

It would be helpful for your child's teacher to know how homework fits into your child's daily schedule. Please complete the homework card by writing down how your child typically spends time in the weekday hours when not in school (e.g., homework, sports practices, music lessons, visitation with noncustodial parents, dinner, sleep, play, TV, computer).

	Monday	Tuesday	Wednesday	Thursday
3:00–4:00 p.m.				
4:00–5:00 p.m.				
5:00–6:00 p.m.				
6:00–7:00 p.m.				
7:00–8:00 p.m.				
8:00–9:00 p.m.				
9:00–10:00 p.m.				
10:00–11:00 p.m.				

FIGURE 2.3
Short Homework Survey for Parents

1. What grade is your child in? _____ What do you feel is an appropriate amount of homework for your child's grade level per evening?

2. How do you feel about weekend homework and homework over holiday vacations?

3. Who is in charge of homework? (Check all that you agree with.)
___ It is the parent's responsibility to make sure the child does homework.
___ Homework is the child's responsibility; parents should not get involved.
___ Parents have the right to excuse their child from homework without penalty for any reason.
___ Parents have the right to excuse their child from homework without penalty if it interferes with the child's sleep, health, or emotional well-being.
___ Parents have the right to excuse their child from homework without penalty if it conflicts with outside activities or family activities.

4. How much control should parents have over the amount and type of homework their child has? (Check all that you agree with.)
___ Parents should be able to request a limit on the *amount* of homework.
___ Parents should be able to request a limit on the *time spent* on homework.
___ Parents should be able to request *modifications* in the difficulty of assignments.
___ Parents should be able to request *additional* homework for their child.
___ The amount and type of homework is up to the teacher.

5. How involved are you with your child's homework? (Check all that apply to you.)
___ I don't get involved in my child's homework.
___ I check to see that my child's homework is done.
___ I have corrected my child's mistakes on homework.
___ I explain things that my child doesn't understand.
___ I help my child study for tests.
___ I have completed homework for my child just to get it done.
___ I sometimes have trouble helping my child because I don't understand the directions.
___ I sometimes have trouble helping my child because I don't understand the material.

___ I'm not sure *how much* I should help my child with homework.

___ I have occasionally prohibited my child from doing homework because it interfered with sleep or family time.

Other_____

A parent feedback checklist (shown in Figure 2.4) can be used as a cover sheet for homework assignments. This checklist provides for two-way communication by allowing teachers to specify the amount of time a child should spend on an assignment and by giving parents options to check if the child is unable to finish the assignment. A student version of the same checklist appears in Chapter 5.

FIGURE 2.4
Parent Feedback Checklist

Dear Parent:

I estimate your child can complete this assignment in _____ minutes.
It is not necessary for your child to work longer than _____ minutes on this assignment, even if he or she does not finish it. Your child will not be penalized.

How much time did your child spend on this assignment? _____
If your child did not finish the assignment, please check the reason or reasons below:

___ My child could no longer focus on the task.

___ My child was too tired.

___ My child did not understand the assignment.

___ My child did not have the necessary materials to complete the assignment.

___ My child did not have enough time because of other outside activities.

___ Other reason (please explain):

_____
Parent signature

---

6. Set parents' minds at ease about homework. An effective partnership also requires trust. Many parents have huge trust issues regarding teachers and homework, based on their past experience or the experiences of other parents. Some parents are afraid that talking to the teacher about homework will be ineffective or even harmful, which is understandable after hearing parent stories such as these:

> I've tried talking to my son's teacher about how he struggles with homework, but whatever I end up talking to her about, she uses it against my son the very next day and embarrasses him publicly. (From the mother of a 5th grader)

> At first I would write notes to the teacher telling her how my daughter wasn't able to finish because it was too much work. But my daughter would get benched at recess time. (From the mother of a 3rd grader)

A lot of anxiety has been created as such stories of teacher retribution are circulated among parents. Most teachers and administrators would be stunned by these stories, but unfortunately there are plenty to go around. Therefore, it is necessary for schools to establish ground rules so that parents feel comfortable talking to teachers about homework.

Again, school officials should work with parent groups to craft a schoolwide zero-tolerance policy stating that there will be no retribution, punishment, or embarrassment of students who do not complete homework. Also included in that policy should be a stipulation that students cannot be failed because of incomplete homework. (These ideas are discussed further in Chapters 4 and 5.)

7. Endorse a set of inalienable homework rights. As an additional sign of good faith, school leaders may wish to go one step further and adopt a set of homework rights for parents and children. Figure 2.5 is an example of a homework rights policy.

FIGURE 2.5
A Bill of Rights for Homework

1. Children shall not be required to work more than 40 hours a week, when class time is added to homework time.

2. Children shall have the right to homework they can complete without help. If they cannot complete homework without help, children shall be entitled to reteaching or modified assignments.

3. A child's academic grade shall not be put in jeopardy because of incomplete homework. Children shall be entitled to an in-school or after-school home-work support program if they are unwilling or unable to complete homework at home.

4. A child's right to playtime, downtime, and adequate sleep shall not be infringed upon by homework.

5. Parents shall be entitled to excuse their child from homework that the child does not understand or is too tired to finish.

6. Families shall be entitled to weekends and holidays free from homework.

Summing Up

Because parents today are from different social and economic classes and have a variety of parenting styles and beliefs about the value of homework, traditional practices related to home-work must be reexamined in light of that diversity. The power relationship between schools and parents must be realigned to embrace parents as equal partners in their child's education. The role of parents in homework must be voluntary, respectful, and individualized, and the value of family life must be honored.

Homework Research and Common Sense

What does the research say about homework, and how should we use that knowledge in making decisions about homework? As we examine the research on homework, it is important to understand the complexity of the process of homework, the limitations of the research, and the simplistic view of learning behind much of the research. Before using homework research to make educational decisions, it is important to first view the research through a critical lens.

A Complicated Practice

One would hope that the outcome of any instructional strategy, including homework, would be to improve learning. The problem is that homework involves the complex interaction of a number of factors (Cooper, 1989a; Corno, 1996; Horsley & Walker, 2013). Educators know that differences exist in children, teachers, tasks, home environments, and measurements of learning, and that the interaction of homework and classroom learning is unique to individual students.

When we try to relate homework to achievement, things get messy. It's difficult to separate where the effect of classroom teaching ends and the effect of homework begins. We don't know how to tease out the effect of homework from prior learning or what occurred in the classroom. We don't know if the same child would have scored just as well on the test *without* doing the homework, or how much better the child scored *because* of doing the homework.

Homework research is especially problematic because we're attempting to study the effect of something that happens out of our sight and out of our control. Unlike classroom learning, we cannot be present when the homework is being done. We don't know whether it was done alone, done with help from others, or downloaded from the Internet. We can't watch it, we can't intervene in the middle of it, and we're not even sure who did it! Because children differ and the conditions under which homework is completed differ, researchers are, in a sense, drawing conclusions blind.

What Homework Researchers Choose to Study

Researchers choose to study and correlate specific factors about the homework process. What they choose to study reflects misperceptions about learning, a simplistic view of factors that explain poor student performance—and therefore what factors should be manipulated to improve academic achievement. Homework researchers often ignore student and teacher differences, focus primarily on time, discount the home, and rely on tests as the sole indicators of learning. Homework, like learning, is very individual—yet researchers attempt to draw blanket conclusions, reflecting the myopic view that all students learn the same thing in the same way.

The body of research on homework paints a curious yet familiar picture of traditional views of education. The research is predominantly about the following elements:

- *Time, not task* (reflecting the belief that more time is the answer to improving education)

- *Groups of students, not individuals* (reflecting a failure to recognize individual differences)
- *Student behavior, not teacher behavior* (reflecting the deficit model—that when children don't learn, the problem lies with them, not the quality of teaching)

Seldom do the studies factor in the role of good teaching or adaptations that teachers make for individual students. This picture is in sharp contrast to the current body of research about learning (Hattie, 2012) and the methods of more progressive educators— methods that reflect the importance of authentic and relevant learning tasks, the need to differentiate, and the belief that all children can learn once teaching methods are matched to their needs.

> Our current "scientific method" focuses almost exclusively on identifying what works best "generally." . . . Children differ. Therein lies what worries me about "evidence based" policy making in education. Good teaching, effective teaching, is not just about using whatever science says "usually" works best. It is all about finding out what works best for the individual child and the group of children in front of you. (Allington, 2005, p. 462)

General Findings of the Research on Homework

Do homework assignments improve achievement? The attempts of researchers to answer this basic question have led to conclusions that are inconsistent at best and contradictory at worst (Horsley & Walker, 2013; Kohn, 2006, 2015). For almost every specific result shown, another study can be found that contradicts the result. Homework has generated enough research that a study can be found to support almost any position, as long as conflicting studies are ignored. Both sides of the homework debate—pro-homework and anti-homework—can cite isolated studies that support their position (Abeles, 2015; Collins &

Bempechat, 2017; Cooper, 2007). Because the influences on homework are complex and subject to interpretation, scholars with opposing views have even used the same research to draw opposite conclusions! Almost any thesis about homework can be "proven" with statistics. Most of us remember little from our college statistics course, leaving us somewhat clueless as researchers attempt to prove their point with *effect sizes, stem and leaf tables,* and results deemed *statistically significant.* So when we read the following research findings, we must examine the evidence cautiously and view the results skeptically.

The following are the major findings of the homework research.

Finding #1: The amount of time spent doing homework is positively correlated with achievement. Most of the homework research falls into one of two research designs. The first type, experimental or quasi-experimental, typically compares groups of students who received homework with groups of students who did not receive homework. Studies comparing students doing homework with students not doing homework showed that the former had higher unit test scores than 73 percent of the latter (Cooper, 2007). The caveat here, noted by the esteemed researcher John Hattie, is that "introducing nearly any innovation is better than its absence" (2009, p. 18).

The second type of research design, represented by a large majority of the homework studies, examines the relationship between time spent on homework and achievement (Cooper, 2007; Fan, Xu, Cai, He, & Fan, 2017). The majority of the studies found a weak but positive correlation between time spent doing homework and achievement (Bas, Senturk, & Cigerci, 2017; Cooper, 2007; Eren & Henderson, 2011; Fernández-Alonso, Suárez-Álvarez, & Muñiz, 2015). That is, as time spent on homework increases, achievement increases. Other studies, however, found the relationship between homework and achievement to be inconsistent or negative—that more time spent on homework was associated with *lower* achievement (Fan et al., 2017; Horsley & Walker, 2013; Maltese, Tai, & Fan, 2012).

Finding #2: Homework appears to be more effective for older students than younger students. Homework appears to be positively correlated with achievement, but the effect size varies dramatically with grade level. In grades 3 to 5, the correlation was nearly zero; in grades 6 to 9, the correlation was .07; and in grades 10 to 12, the correlation was .25 (Cooper, 1989a; Cooper, Robinson, & Patall, 2006). Remember that 1.00 is a perfect correlation between two measures and zero means there is no correlation between two measures.

How is achievement measured in these studies? When studies correlate time spent on homework with achievement, achievement is usually measured by one of three types of data: scores on teacher-designed tests, grades given by teachers, or scores on standardized tests (Horsley & Walker, 2013; Kohn, 2006). Cooper's meta-analysis of homework studies (Cooper, 1989b; Cooper et al., 1998; Cooper et al., 2006) combined studies with all three types of achievement measures to reach his cumulative correlations (described earlier) about time and achievement.

When those measures of achievement were viewed separately, Cooper and colleagues (2006) indicated that class grades (either general grades or grades on tests) showed slightly higher correlations with homework than did standardized tests, but that the difference in the two types of achievement was not significant. Maltese and colleagues (2012) reached a different conclusion: in their study of high school math and science students, they found no consistent relationship between homework and grades but a positive relationship between homework and standardized test scores.

Finding #3: As more variables are controlled for, the correlation between homework and achievement diminishes. Unfortunately, simply correlating time and achievement ignores many other variables that may affect achievement. The work of

Keith and his colleagues is significant because they conducted research with large numbers of high school students. The discrepancy between their original research and their follow-up research is particularly revealing (see Cool & Keith, 1991; Keith, 1982; Keith & Cool, 1992). In their original research,

> Cool and Keith (1991) found a positive correlation between time spent on homework and achievement ($r = +0.30$). After controlling for motivation, ability, quality of instruction, course work quantity, and some background variables, however, no meaningful effect of homework on achievement remained. (Trautwein & Koller, 2003, p. 121)

Maltese and colleagues (2012), studying high school math and science students, controlled for student background, motivation, and prior achievement, and found the following:

> The results clearly indicate that *Time on homework* does not have a significant association with *Final grade* in these analyses and there is no substantive difference in grades between students who complete homework and those who do not. These results do not seem to support the positive association seen in most published research. (p. 61)

It appears that much of the correlation between time and achievement could be a result of the ability level of the student, the quality of instruction, or how rigorous the course was. Does homework cause higher achievement, or do high achievers spend more time on homework? Are higher-ability students more likely to take more challenging courses that require more homework (Horsley & Walker, 2013)?

Due to such discrepancies and other flaws in homework studies, researchers disagree as to whether homework enhances achievement. Whereas many hold strongly to their assertion that homework is beneficial (Collins & Bempechat, 2017; Cooper, 2007), others point to newer studies that seem to discount early research (Abeles, 2015; Bennett & Kalish, 2006; Kohn, 2006, 2015). A new generation of homework studies using more sophisticated analyses often fail to find a significant relationship between homework and achievement (Horsley & Walker, 2013).

Finding #4: At each grade level, there appears to be an optimum amount of homework. "There is no evidence that any amount of homework improves the academic performance of elementary school students" (Cooper, 1989a, p. 109). Does this mean there is no value in homework at the elementary level? Not necessarily. Several explanations for Cooper's conclusion are possible. First, younger students have less developed academic skills and shorter attention spans, and they require more adult assistance in learning, so working independently may be less productive. It is also possible that academic performance is difficult to measure at this age or that academic growth is slow and uneven. Even though the research cannot show a correlation, common sense suggests that time spent reading would improve reading skills, or that time spent practicing math facts would improve math skills. Perhaps this is why some researchers—despite the data and the growing belief among educators that there is no benefit to homework in elementary school—often recommend that young children be given small amounts of homework.

For middle school students (grades 6 through 9), research shows that achievement improves slightly with even a minimal amount of homework (less than one hour). In other words, even a small amount of reinforcement of classroom learning seems beneficial. Achievement continues to improve until assignments last between one and two hours a night. Homework requiring more time than that is no longer associated with higher achievement (Cooper et al., 2006; Cooper, 2007).

That said, Eren and Henderson (2011) arrived at an interesting finding after collecting data on 25,000 8th graders who were doing an average of about two hours of homework nightly, all subjects combined. The researchers found that adding another 15 minutes a night of *math* homework correlated with an approximately 3 percent gain in test scores, but that additional homework in English, science, and social studies had little or no effect on test scores in those subjects.

For high school students (grades 10 through 12), achievement appears to improve until students are doing about two hours of homework a night. At that point, achievement begins to decline (Cooper et al., 2006). "Correlational evidence suggests that high school students doing more than about two hours of homework a night achieve no better than those doing about two hours, and maybe worse" (Cooper, 2007, p. 37). The correlations with larger amounts of homework for middle and high school students seem logical, because older students are better able to work independently and for longer periods. One would hope that older students have also honed their study skills over the years. However, a study of more than 7,000 adolescents in Spain found that 70 minutes a night was the threshold for effectiveness; after that, achievement flatlined or declined (American Psychological Association, 2015; Fernández-Alonso et al., 2015).

The gist of the research, then, is that a small amount of homework may be good for learning, but too much homework can actually be bad for learning. There appears to be a curvilinear relationship between homework and achievement—that is, up to a point, homework appears positive, but past the optimum amount, achievement either remains flat or declines (Cooper, 2007; Fernández-Alonso et al., 2015). Children as well as adults have a limit to how much mental work they can accomplish in a day's time before the brain needs downtime and time to process information (Jensen, 2000).

Curiously, the research about the appropriate amount of homework for different grade levels is consistent with an informal guideline that many teachers already practice. Both the National Education Association (NEA) and the Parent Teacher Association

(PTA) have long endorsed what is called "the 10-minute rule" (origin unknown). The 10-minute rule states that the maximum amount of nightly homework should not exceed 10 minutes per grade level per night, all subjects combined. In other words, a 1st grader should have no more than 10 minutes of homework per night, a 6th grader no more than 60 minutes per night, and a 12th grader no more than 120 minutes per night. Those time limits are reflected in the curvilinear relationship Cooper and others noted—when the amount of time spent exceeds the 10-minute rule, a leveling out or decline in achievement is observed.

Finding #5: Homework is less effective than many other instructional strategies. In 2009, John Hattie published *Visible Learning*, possibly the most exhaustive compilation of educational research ever. In it, he synthesizes more than 800 meta-analyses relating to student achievement and what works in schools. He notes:

> Instead of asking "What works?" we should be asking "What works best?" as the answers to these two questions are quite different . . . the answer to the first question is "Almost everything" whereas the answer to the second is more circumscribed—and some things work better and some work worse relative to the many possible alternatives. (Hattie, 2009, p. 18)

Hattie (2009) rank-ordered 138 influences on learning (as diverse as socioeconomic status, class size, and small-group learning) based on their statistical effect size. Those ranked highest were determined to have the largest influence on learning, whereas those ranked lowest had the smallest effect on learning. Interestingly, *homework* ranked 88th, yet *feedback*, a purpose uniquely suited to homework, ranked 10th! All homework can be used as feedback if the teacher chooses to use it that way, provided the task and conditions are right. Ideally, however, feedback occurs regularly in the classroom as well. (Homework as feedback is discussed in greater detail in Chapter 4.)

Hattie's synthesis reaffirms Cooper's findings on the differences of homework's effectiveness across grade levels, but his interpretation of a broader body of homework research led to this conclusion: "Prescribing homework does not help students develop time management skills—there is no evidence this occurs" (Hattie, 2009, p. 235).

Limitations of the Research

The findings of the research on homework are limited by at least three important considerations: the overreliance on the work of one researcher and his colleagues, general quality of homework research, and individual differences among students.

Overreliance on Cooper's Work

Given the limited number of large-scale studies and the many smaller isolated studies that show conflicting results, it is difficult to draw reliable conclusions. As a result, we are forced to rely heavily on the work of one researcher and his colleagues—the only researchers to conduct any significant syntheses of the large number of studies. Dr. Harris Cooper of Duke University is widely regarded as the nation's leading researcher on homework. Cooper, along with numerous colleagues, has conducted and published several compilations and meta-analyses of homework over the last 30 years (Cooper, 1989a, 1989b, 1994, 2001, 2007; Cooper et al., 2006; Cooper & Valentine, 2001), but none in the last 10 years or so. Although more recent studies exist that are not included in his meta-analyses, his synthesis is probably the most useful for examining the research on homework. This situation leaves us in the dubious position of relying solely on one source of interpretation of the research—much like getting one's daily view of world events solely from one television network or newspaper.

Although Cooper's syntheses of homework research have been extensive, his reviews are uncritical. He simply combines the results of similar studies, performs statistical analyses, draws conclusions, and makes recommendations. At certain points after drawing conclusions, he may state a caveat relating to sample size or other factors, but his work is primarily statistical analysis, not a critique of the quality of the research (Cooper, 2007). Despite this shortcoming, Cooper is the researcher most often cited when writers make recommendations about homework.

General Quality of Homework Research

As critical consumers, it is important to scrutinize not only Cooper's methodology but also the pervasive flaws in the homework research as a whole, which include the following:

- Many studies rely on self-reporting by students or parents as to how much time was spent on homework.
- Time spent on homework is measured as the cumulative time spent per week, not by the day.
- Sample sizes of students may be as small as a few students or a few classrooms.
- Often students are not randomly assigned to groups.
- Some studies measure homework assigned, not homework completed.
- Measures of achievement are inconsistent across studies (e.g., the measure may be test grades, standardized test scores, homework grades based on completion, or homework grades based on accuracy).

Aren't All Students Different?

In many of the research studies, groups of students are compared with each other (as when one class receives homework and another class does not). Regardless of attempts to randomize two groups of students, individual differences will still persist (Vatterott, 2017). Each student constructs meaning and understands concepts in his or her own unique way (Tomlinson, 2014a). Therefore, it is impossible to know what variations in achievement might be the result of differences in individual students as opposed to differences in the treatment. Homework could be effective with one student or set of students but not another for an infinite number of reasons, such as the quality of the task, students' prior knowledge, working conditions, amount of help at home, or even how well students paid attention in class that day!

A Commonsense Look at the Research

Taking a commonsense look at the research involves considering several aspects that may be problematic. These include the measures of time and achievement in the research, the assumptions made about cause and effect, and various caveats related to researcher bias, faulty conclusions, and questionable recommendations.

Common Sense About Time and Achievement

The measures of both time and achievement in the research are problematic. Just as educational reformers focus on extending the school day or the school year, homework researchers seem to be caught in the "seat time equals education" metaphor, as if more time is the answer. Remember that in most studies, time is measured as the cumulative amount of time spent per week, which tells us nothing about the frequency of the assignments (Hattie, 2009; Trautwein, Koller, Schmitz, & Baumert, 2002). Remember, too, that measurements of time spent are usually self-reports by students.

Most studies don't consider that different students have different "working speeds" (Goldberg, 2012; Trautwein & Koller, 2003). More time spent on homework could indicate a slower working speed, or simply that those students complete all the homework assigned. Lumping together students who work at various speeds into one statistical profile renders the results questionable. When the research focuses on *time* instead of *task*, it fails to take into account which types of learning tasks contribute most significantly to learning. Time is simply not a valid metric (Horsley & Walker, 2013).

Enlightened educators realized long ago that simply providing more time did not, by itself, produce more learning. Although time is a factor in learning, and engaged time is a necessity, children differ in the time they take to complete a learning task (Guskey & Jung 2013; Vatterott, 2015). The learning that is accomplished is more important than how much time it takes. Learning is not a *Jeopardy!* game, in which people are judged by how fast they can access the answer, or an academic race where people are judged on how many facts they can recite in five minutes.

For individual learners, it makes sense that more time spent would equal more learning. Then why would some studies show that *more* time spent on homework is correlated with *lower* achievement? Those studies may be reflecting results for students with less prior knowledge or students with slower working speeds. When comparing slower processors with faster processors, the student who works more slowly could spend more time on homework and still perform poorly on tests (Cooper & Valentine, 2001; Vatterott, 2015).

Using teacher-made tests, grades, or standardized test scores to measure achievement is also problematic. Scores on standardized tests are least likely to be influenced by homework and are most likely to correlate with the affluence and educational level of parents (Kohn, 2000). Although teacher-made tests or grades may yield a correlation with homework, much research exists to refute the faulty logic that those measures actually indicate that learning has taken place (Guskey & Jung, 2013; O'Connor, 2013). Teacher-made tests and grades reflect many things other than learning, such as the ability to memorize well, turn homework in on time, follow rules, and behave properly. Teachers are increasingly realizing the limitations of traditional tests to measure learning, causing many of them to move to performance-based assessments.

Common Sense About Cause and Effect

Correlation is not causation (Hattie, 2009; Horsley & Walker, 2013). Just because high-achieving students do more homework does not mean that doing more homework *causes* higher achievement. It is just as likely that high-achieving students are good at homework and therefore do more of it. Yet many researchers attempt to infer causation when making recommendations based on their research. Alfie Kohn (2006) uses a colorful example to make this point:

> Statistical principles don't get much more basic than "correlation doesn't prove causation." The number of umbrellas brought to a workplace on a given morning will be highly correlated with the probability of precipitation in the afternoon, but the presence of the umbrellas didn't *make* it rain. . . . Nevertheless, most research purporting to show a positive effect of homework seems to be based on the assumption that when students who get (or do) more homework also score better on standardized tests, it follows that the higher scores were due to their having had more homework. (p. 28)

Beware of Researcher Bias

The conclusion of many researchers that homework *causes* higher achievement should be the equivalent of a large yellow caution sign reading "BEWARE OF RESEARCHER BIAS" or "*Proceed with caution: Results may be tainted by the researcher's inherent belief in the goodness of homework.*"

Conclusions of homework researchers cannot be divorced from their biases. Two people can do a meta-analysis and still draw two different conclusions due to their bias for or against homework. The homework research is rife with examples of conclusions not supported by the data and recommendations that go far beyond what is justified by the conclusions.

A good analogy is the researcher bias that is evident in medical research. For example, older studies of heart disease studied only men yet made blanket recommendations for heart health of both men and women. Studies touting the effectiveness of specific drugs have been questioned when it was discovered that the studies were financed by the company that manufactures the drug.

Beware of Conclusions That Don't Match Results

We must use research to inform yet have a healthy skepticism for what must naturally be a flawed process. Statistics being what they are, the same data can be extrapolated in different ways to present different and confusing results. Take, for instance, Cooper's data on the relationship between grade level and achievement. His research shows that the correlation of time spent on homework and achievement is higher at higher grade levels. In 2001, Cooper wrote this:

> For high school students (grades 10–12), a sizable average correlation was found ($r = +.25$), whereas for students in grades 6–9, the average correlation was small ($r = +.07$), and for elementary school students, it was nearly nonexistent ($r = +.02$). (p. 26)

In 2007, Cooper combined the data differently:

> We grouped correlations into those involving elementary students (grades kindergarten–6) and those involving secondary school students (grades 7–12). This was the best we could do given the precision of the data. The average correlation between time spent on homework and achievement was substantial for secondary school students, averaging about +.25 across 23 samples. For elementary school

students, it hovered around zero for the average of 10 samples. (pp. 29–30)

This interpretation makes it appear that students in grades 7–9
benefited as much from homework as students in grades 10–12,
a stark contrast to the earlier analysis that separated the data
into the two groups.

Conclusions that don't match results often begin with "however" or "although":

> However, even though no significant differences between
> grade levels were found in this research, academic achieve-
> ment scores of students tended to rise as the grade level
> went up. *So, it may be concluded that homework works well in
> upper grade levels* [emphasis added]. (Bas et al., 2017, p. 40)

Really?! I don't think so.

Beware of Recommendations That Don't Match Conclusions

Just as we teach our students to be critical consumers of
information and not to believe everything they read on the
Internet, educators must be critical consumers of research as
well. Research must always be examined carefully to determine
its quality, its relevance, the logic of its conclusions, and whether
the recommendations made are consistent with the conclusions
of the study.

As mentioned previously, Cooper (1989a) concluded that
"there is no evidence that any amount of homework improves
the academic performance of elementary school students" (p.
109). Marzano and Pickering (2007) cited that research as well.
But the "innate goodness" of homework is so ingrained, researchers often don't see their own bias. Both Cooper and Marzano,
after stating that the research shows no benefit of homework for
elementary students, nonetheless proceed to recommend homework for elementary students. Cooper (2016) continues to claim

it should be given for the purpose of developing good study habits and positive attitudes—a recommendation not backed by any
research (Weir, 2016).

Many researchers have such clearly ingrained biases toward
homework that they don't appear to see the disconnect between
the research they are citing and the recommendations they are
making. In fact, the pro-homework bias is so prevalent, researchers who find a *negative* correlation between homework and
achievement often tend to discount the results:

> Researchers who report this counterintuitive finding gen-
> erally take pains to explain that it "must not be interpreted
> as a causal pattern." . . . How rare it is to find these same
> cautions about the misleading nature of correlational results
> when those results suggest a *positive* relationship between
> homework and achievement. It's only when the outcome
> doesn't fit the expected pattern (and support the case for
> homework) that it's carefully explained away. (Kohn, 2006,
> pp. 29–30)

In an interesting twist of fate, Cooper's research that people once
used to justify homework is now being used to justify eliminating
homework at the elementary level.

Should We Ignore the Research Altogether?

As we see the mismatches between research results and recommendations inherent in the homework research, we may wonder if there is any value in the research at all. Should we ignore
the research altogether? No. Common sense tells us otherwise.
The value of the research is in the broad strokes it paints, not
in the minutiae. Its value comes as we reflect on the *logic* of its
conclusions—do they make sense for *our* population of students?
Are they consistent with what we have come to know from experience about our type and age of student? The other value of
research is to dispel the myths behind some of the most strongly

held beliefs about homework discussed in Chapter 1. We must remind ourselves that we're still not sure exactly how learning happens within different students and how much individuals differ in their learning needs.

Common Sense: 10 Things Teachers Know About Learning

Given the limitations of the research on homework, it would be easy to feel that we have no good compass to guide us in our use of homework. But that is not true—we have two very powerful bodies of knowledge that are germane to the decisions we make about homework.

First, much research exists about how children learn and the factors that influence learning. Research about the brain, time on task, motivation, persistence, and learner differences offer valuable insights into the design of homework tasks that support classroom learning.

Second, our own personal experience as teachers and administrators provides a wealth of information and perspective. Our experience has taught us much, especially if we have been reflective in our practice and have learned from others during our tenure. Experience has honed our common sense about teaching and learning. That common sense about education is really nothing more than our instincts and intuition about what works and what doesn't work. That common sense may be more valuable (and is definitely more accessible) than all the research in the world. We can use what we already know from our own classroom experiences to guide our choices about homework.

In contrast to the widespread myths about homework discussed in Chapter 1, the truth is that several tenets about learning exist that directly affect the practice of homework in anyone's classroom. These tenets are explored briefly in this chapter and form the rationale for effective homework practices recommended in Chapters 4 and 5.

Tenet #1: Quality Teaching Matters

Common sense tells us that the effectiveness or ineffectiveness of classroom teaching must greatly influence homework (Hattie, 2009, 2012). Homework is just one piece of the teaching-learning picture, one that is highly regulated by the teacher and, one would hope, connected to what happens in the classroom. What if, instead of focusing on the *student's* homework behavior, we looked at the *teacher's* homework behavior? Have we considered the possibility that some teachers might use homework more *effectively,* might do more diagnosing and individualizing of homework? What if effective teachers provided more *appropriate* homework, homework that children might find worthwhile and enjoyable? One thing we know is that classroom organization, a teacher's homework habits, and attitudes and method of feedback all influence the effectiveness of homework (Hattie, 2009; Horsley & Walker, 2013). One group of researchers speculated about the connection between teacher behaviors and homework:

> Teachers who assign a lot of homework might differ from other teachers in nontrivial respects. Their lessons might be less organized, meaning that they have to assign more of the workload as homework. Another difference may lie in their teaching styles: Teachers who assign a lot of homework may tend to assign the kind of homework that does not support learning in the best possible way. (Trautwein et al., 2002, p. 45)

Organization and structure of the learning process. How the teacher clarifies learning objectives, organizes content, scaffolds learning, and checks for understanding all contribute to the quality of learning for individual students. The general learning environment, whether orderly or chaotic, focused or distracting, may or may not be conducive to the effective use of homework (Vatterott, 2015).

Two 3rd Grade Classrooms

In Mrs. Sanders's 3rd grade classroom, the objective for the day's lesson is written on the board, as is tonight's homework assignment. She explains how to multiply two-digit numbers and does a sample problem. She checks for understanding by having students do two sample problems and check with their neighbors. She reminds students to write down the homework assignment and allows them a few minutes to do so, checking on certain students. She gives students 10 minutes to start their homework problems, during which time she walks around the room waiting for questions or confused looks. Zack is unsure about what he's doing. When Mrs. Sanders walks by his desk, he asks for help.

In another 3rd grade classroom, Mrs. Evans begins her lesson by explaining the purpose to the students, but some students are still assembling their materials and not listening. She shows students how to multiply two-digit numbers by doing two problems on the board. She does a third problem by asking the students what to do. A few students raise their hands to explain the steps, but not all students are engaged. She then orally tells students what the homework assignment is and tells them they have 10 minutes to begin their homework in class. Jason was not paying attention when Mrs. Evans gave the assignment and has asked another student what the assignment was. Melanie has trouble with oral instructions and also asks another student. Several students are talking softly to each other, which is distracting to some students who cannot concentrate on the homework. Andrew is confused but doesn't want to bother Mrs. Evans, who is now busy at her desk grading yesterday's homework assignments.

The teacher's homework behavior. The teacher's homework behavior relates to the quality and quantity of homework assigned, the discussing of homework in class, and the methods of checking or grading (Epstein & Van Voorhis, 2001; Núñez et al., 2015). How homework supports a teacher's style of teaching and how much and how often homework is given will greatly affect whether homework is completed. Homework's connection to what happens in the classroom is also important. Is homework used in the classroom to inform lessons, or is it unrelated? When teachers use homework to check for understanding, do they give nonpunitive feedback? Do they reteach concepts students did not understand? All these teacher behaviors will affect how useful homework will be (Vatterott, 2015).

Teacher attitudes about homework. How teachers describe homework tasks to students and how they defend the purpose of homework say a lot about their attitudes. Is the purpose of the homework clearly connected to classroom learning, or is it just to be completed because the teacher said to do it? Is homework viewed as distasteful or used as punishment, or is a "no-homework pass" used as a reward for good behavior? Perception is everything, and students infer a lot from the attitude the teacher displays about homework (Trautwein, Niggli, Schnyder, & Ludtke, 2009). Those attitudes are usually revealed in the rewards and punishments doled out for completing or not completing homework on time (Vatterott, 2015).

How a teacher chooses to give feedback about homework can encourage or discourage a student from completing homework (Núñez et al., 2015). (Feedback and grading are discussed in detail in Chapter 4.) Nonthreatening feedback with no grades attached provides positive information to students and keeps the focus on checking for understanding and learning (Brookhart, 2017). Detailed feedback is more effective than simple numbers or letters. When students receive no feedback on homework, it sends a message that homework is not important and not related to classroom learning. Overly harsh grading or late penalties increase student anxiety, and with older students such penalties often provoke a defiance to not do homework at all (Schimmer, 2012). One group of researchers speculated:

> The combination of a lot of homework and a lack of monitoring seems to indicate a rather ineffective teaching style with respect to learning. In other words, this interaction effect may reflect a generally inefficient teaching style rather than detrimental effects of homework on learning. (Trautwein et al., 2002, p. 43)

A teacher's comments and facial expressions in reaction to homework also send powerful messages. If a student does a homework assignment incorrectly, does the teacher blame the student for not paying attention or not working hard enough— "You must not have been listening when I explained it" or "Why did you do it this way?" (The student hears "What an idiot you are!")—or does he say something like "Oh, I guess my explanation didn't click—let's go over it again," reassuring the student that, in this classroom, it is safe to make mistakes?

Tenet #2: Skills Require Practice

Teachers know that certain learning skills require practice to perfect, and often homework is used for practice. Research confirms that mastering a skill requires focused practice (Hattie, 2012; Hattie & Yates, 2014), but there are many conditions under which that practice may occur. First, we must make sure students are practicing the skill correctly, so they do not internalize incorrect methods (Hattie, 2009; Trautwein & Koller, 2003).

Two Methods of Practice

Mr. Johnson demonstrates the steps in multiplying fractions and does two sample problems on the board. He then assigns 20 problems for homework practice. Susan correctly understood the steps and completes all 20 problems correctly. Sam, however, misunderstood and does all 20 problems incorrectly, practicing the *incorrect* way of multiplying fractions. Sam has great difficulty relearning the correct way later.

Mrs. Hernandez uses a different method. She demonstrates the steps and does sample problems. She then has everyone do problems in class and discuss what they did with their neighbor. She gives two-part math homework assignments. Part 1 asks students to explain the steps in the new process they have just learned and to do only three problems. (These she checks for understanding the next day.) Part 2 includes several practice problems of a process that students learned a few weeks ago. These are practice problems for a process she is sure they now understand and can do correctly.

Second, we must give students adequate time to practice before we assume they have internalized the skill correctly (Wright, 2006). Mrs. Hernandez's method (just described) is preferable because it allows for corrective feedback and the shaping of the skill that is practiced. Frequently teachers rush prematurely into a heavy practice phase, without adequately checking for understanding. A wiser approach would be to examine a few problems in depth and focus on the reasoning used to solve them before moving to the stage of practice (Marzano, 2010).

Third, an approach that uses smaller amounts of practice spread out over a number of days (distributed practice) is superior to one that uses larger amounts of practice done over a shorter period (mass practice). Shorter, more frequent periods of practice are better than longer assignments given less frequently (Hattie, 2009, 2012).

Tenet #3: Time on Task Matters

Teachers know that more time on task helps learning and that homework is one way to gain more time for students to learn. We also know that some students need more time to process and internalize information. Suppose we tell all students to study for a test for 30 minutes. Will all students achieve the same results in 30 minutes? No—because there is a difference between the amount of time *spent on learning* and the amount of time *needed to learn* (Hattie, 2009; Vatterott, 2015). Time *needed to learn* is influenced by aptitude, ability to understand instruction, and the quality of instruction (Carr, 2013; Trautwein & Koller, 2003). As many of us remember from our own experience as students, one student may study four times as long as another student, and both will earn the same grade on the test (Bryan & Burstein, 2004).

When all students are given a homework task of the same length, students who need more time to learn are at a disadvantage. An assignment that may take Amanda 30 minutes to complete may take Ben 90 minutes. If Ben is a high school student with homework in multiple subjects, he may need more time to learn than is available to him during nonschool hours. The dilemma then becomes how we provide those students with that extra time without overburdening them.

For students who need more time to learn, teachers will find it necessary to prioritize work or limit the number of standards that individual students are expected to master (Guskey & Jung, 2013; Vatterott, 2015). This is a common practice for special education students, but it may be necessary for other students as well. By prioritizing homework in specific subjects and reducing the length of homework assignments, it is possible to give students adequate time to learn. (More options for extending the amount of time students have for homework are discussed in Chapter 5.)

Time on task refers to teachers, too. They need adequate time to plan effective classroom activities. What if more time spent grading homework equaled less time to plan quality classroom instruction, which could affect the quality and amount of learning that occurs in the classroom?

Tenet #4: Task Is as Important as Time

The quality of the homework task is as important as the amount of time required (Anderson, 2016; Vatterott, 2014, 2015). Students make decisions about whether to attempt homework based on their assessment of the task. Is the homework perceived to be interesting or boring, simple or tedious (Bennett, 2017)? Students are less likely to complete tasks they perceive as busywork. Quality homework tasks allow students to practice or process information, introduce them to material that will be discussed in the future, or provide feedback to teachers so they may check for understanding. Quality tasks are clearly related to classroom learning, are simple enough that students can complete them without help, and, it is hoped, are relevant to real life (Vatterott, 2010). (Examples of quality homework tasks are presented in greater detail in Chapter 4.)

Tenet #5: Learning Is Individual

Teachers know that each student is unique and that everyone learns differently (Dueck, 2014; Tomlinson, 2014a). A basic concern about the homework research is that it reports on *averages*. The 10-minute rule, for instance, suggests that 10 minutes of homework per grade level per night is the maximum amount of work that should be assigned. But that is an *average*—which means that for some students, the optimum amount will be lower or higher. As Abeles (2015) notes, "The guideline fails to recognize that time spent on a given homework assignment can vary substantially from one child to the next" (p. 75). For instance, some 6th graders may be capable of sustaining attention and benefiting from 60 minutes a night, some may be capable of working 90 minutes a night, and others may have trouble completing just 30 minutes of homework and may not benefit from more.

Because learning is individual, some students learn quickly in the classroom and may not require any practice or reinforcement —but others do. In any case, each student will have an optimum amount of time for doing homework effectively. Some students will need shorter assignments, and some assignments will need to be prioritized for mastery (Carr, 2013).

Homework needs to be personalized to fit the specific needs of individual students (Manninen, 2014). Some students will have less time available, some students will have less supervision, and some students will need more sleep or downtime than other students. (Methods for individualizing homework are discussed in Chapter 4.)

Tenet #6: Children Differ in Readiness and Developmental Level

Whether they are in elementary, middle, or high school, students differ in their level of prior knowledge, the sophistication of their academic skills, and their readiness for new learning. New learning must be scaffolded onto existing frameworks. Students with limited readiness may need more direct instruction, practice, concrete experience, or simpler reading material (Tomlinson, 2014a). More advanced students may benefit from tasks that are more challenging or the opportunity to explore topics in greater depth (Vatterott, 2007, 2010).

Diagnosing individual students' levels of readiness is an important job for teachers (Anderson, 2016; Bryan & Burstein, 2004; Depka, 2015). Homework can initially be used for diagnosis and then adapted to fit individual student needs. "For a teacher, understanding a student's level of development is crucial, as is spotting where, when, and why mistakes are made in learning something new" (Buell, 2004, p. 18).

Common sense tells us that differentiated instruction is necessary and desirable, yet when it comes to homework, teachers often assign the same task to all students, regardless of their level of readiness (Kallick & Zmuda, 2017; Tomlinson, 2014a). (Chapter 4 discusses how homework tasks should be differentiated to meet individual student needs.)

Tenet #7: Children Differ in Learning Preferences

Research on learning modalities, multiple intelligences, and the brain has shown that students have preferences for the way they learn best (Dunn & Honigsfeld, 2013; Gardner, 1999). For instance, learners' preferences may be auditory, visual, tactile, or kinesthetic. Some may require diagrams or schematics, whereas others may learn easily through reading. Some may prefer tasks that allow them to use drawing, music, or bodily movement to express what they have learned or to help them remember information.

Although respecting individual learner differences is important, I do not advise grouping students into discrete categories *solely* according to learning preference. Pigeonholing learners as one "type" is overly simplistic (Willingham, Hughes, & Dobolyi, 2015); we have come to understand that learning is much more complex. Tomlinson (2009) suggests that learning preferences are more fluid than fixed and may vary from subject to subject or even from concept to concept within a subject. What to do instead? Empower students to decide which methods work best for them for specific concepts and skills. By providing choices and flexibility in homework tasks, teachers can accommodate differences in learners and therefore increase the effectiveness of homework (Anderson, 2016; Bryan & Burstein, 2004; Manninen, 2014; Vatterott, 2007).

Homework Geared to Individual Learning Preferences

Miss Lee knew it was important for her 4th graders to know their multiplication tables by memory. The students' homework assignment was to design a method to help them memorize their multiplication tables. She gave them several suggestions, such as writing them, reciting them, or making charts. The students were free to design whatever method they thought would work best for them. Some of the students' methods included writing a rap song, using pictures, making a poster with rows of stickers, and making their own flash cards. Each student was then required to log how much time he or she spent practicing each week. Students shared their methods with their classmates and were allowed to practice using one another's methods.

Tenet #8: Children Differ in Motivation, Persistence, and Organizational Skills

Homework is a classic form of self-regulated learning. Students decide whether, when, and how to tackle the homework tasks they have been assigned (Bennett, 2017; Vatterott, 2014). Children differ in their level of motivation, and that motivation to complete homework is mediated by several factors.

First, students who have a feeling of competence about learning are more likely to do homework. The feeling of competence is influenced by a student's expectation of success, which is based on past experience (Cushman, 2014; Darling-Hammond & Ifill-lynch, 2006; Lin-Siegler, Dweck, & Cohen, 2016). Therefore, students who have an academic history of doing poorly on homework assignments need tasks at which they can be successful. They need positive feedback for completing homework—positive experiences to "undo" the negative experiences of the past (Goldberg, 2012; Vatterott, 2010).

Second, completing homework requires perseverance. Students with a positive self-concept or self-efficacy are more likely to persist when faced with difficult tasks (Sagor, 2008; Vatterott, 2014). Students who lack perseverance may lack strategies. They may ask, "What should I do when I don't understand the assignment?" Students who lack strategies may not think to look back over what they have read or to call a friend for help (Bryan & Burstein, 2004; Carr, 2013). They may lack metacognitive skills such as orienting, planning, executing, monitoring, evaluating, and correcting. A lack of metacognitive skills often leads to students abandoning tasks too easily (Goldberg, 2012; Levine, 2003). Some students, especially students with special needs, give up on tasks rather quickly, having developed "learned helplessness," which is often unwittingly reinforced by family members. Families that supervise homework and value persistence may encourage students to keep working, while other families may not. Motivation and persistence are also influenced by student interests and the value the student attaches to the task (Azzam, 2014; Pink, 2009). Wise teachers seek feedback from students and consider how they might tap into student interests.

Tenet #9: Frustration Is Detrimental to Motivation and Desire to Learn

Some teachers will say that frustration in learning is good and necessary. For the achievement-oriented student who has successfully overcome frustration in the past, that may be true. These students may have a higher tolerance for frustration and therefore be motivated to try harder. But for students who are fearful of failing and being judged, frustration is a cost they may not be willing to pay, especially if they possess no strategies for getting beyond the frustration (Bennett, 2017). Differences in motivation, persistence, and organizational skills oblige teachers to adapt homework assignments to provide opportunities for maximum success and minimum frustration for each student. This obligation means homework assignments should be time based (Goldberg, 2012)—students should be instructed to do as much as they can in a certain number of minutes and given feedback on what they complete. Students who have trouble persisting with difficult tasks must be given work that is doable and receive one-on-one assistance (Darling-Hammond & Ifill-Lynch, 2006; Depka, 2015). Their homework should be monitored more closely, with an emphasis on progress and with improvement noted (Núñez et al., 2015). They must be taught concrete strategies, assigned study buddies, or provided after-school support programs. (All these remedies are discussed in Chapters 4 and 5.) For students who have difficulty persisting with homework, checking for frustration is as critical as checking for understanding.

Checking for Frustration

Mrs. Johnson asks her 2nd graders to write the number of minutes they spent on each homework assignment at the top of the page. She also has three circle faces at the top of the assignment—one smiling, one neutral, and one frowning. Students circle a face to describe their level of understanding of the assignment: "I got this,"

"I've got some questions," or "I'm totally frustrated!" Mrs. Johnson uses this feedback to check for learner frustration and to adjust the difficulty of assignments for specific students.

Tenet #10: Homework That Is Not Completed Doesn't Help Learning

We know that if homework is not completed, it doesn't help anything. Assigning homework does no good if students don't do it. By contrast, well-designed homework that students complete successfully can reinforce classroom learning and allow for additional time on task.

Summing Up

The homework research is a cautionary tale, not a hard-and-fast prescription for action. We want to know what the research says, but it is not prudent to be a slave to the numbers. The inability of research to prove homework's usefulness does not mean that homework *cannot* be useful or worthwhile; it just shows that homework *has not* been useful in many cases. The research does not validate the love affair some teachers seem to have with homework. If we choose to give homework, we should do so very carefully. We should reflect carefully about its purpose, plan the nature of the task carefully, and assess homework carefully to check for understanding.

Our own classroom experience provides much common sense about how to coordinate classroom learning and homework in a way that uses homework effectively. Many experienced teachers would maintain that teaching is more art than science, and although the science of research may inform our actions, it must not dictate them. The needs of individual learners must be the driving force behind all instructional decisions. Children are not seeds in a petri dish or rats in a maze. They are dynamic, thinking, feeling human beings, each with unique learning needs.

Learning is a complex process that, despite all our research, we still struggle to understand. Chapter 4 discusses how to create quality homework tasks that will support classroom learning for individual students.

Effective Homework Practices

Chapters 4 and 5 bring us to the question most teachers want answered: "How can I get them to do their homework?" (Darling-Hammond & Ifill-Lynch, 2006). We tend to look for the quick fix—expressing concern more about "How can we *make* them do their homework?" instead of looking more deeply at "Why *don't* they do their homework?" The search for answers is a complex one that requires us to conduct a methodical examination. Many strategies exist to improve the rate of homework completion, but before discussing those strategies, we must rethink how common practices may contribute to the problem. We must look at the old paradigm of how we *do* homework and suggest a new paradigm.

Rethinking Common Homework Practices: The Old Paradigm

The old homework paradigm is a set of common practices driven by the traditional beliefs and attitudes that were discussed in Chapter 1. The paradigm is built upon such ideas as the belief in the inherent goodness of homework, the assumption that the homework is doable and any problems are related to motivation, the belief that the key to controlling student behavior lies in reward and punishment, and the attitude that homework should be completed simply because the teacher told the student to do it.

Chapter 3 revealed what common sense and experience tell us about learners. Despite what teachers know from experience about learners and learning, when it comes to homework, common sense is often not reflected in common practice. For instance, we know that students differ in their readiness and developmental level and that all students do not learn in the same way, yet homework is often one-size-fits-all, with all students being assigned the same task (Dueck, 2014; Eisner, 2003–2004).

We know that students differ in their "working speed"—that some take longer to learn a concept or complete tasks than others—yet teachers often expect students who work more slowly to take the additional time to complete the same homework task that other students finish more quickly. The remedy often is to give the child *more time* instead of *less work* (Goldberg, 2012). Homework completion is often task based, regardless of how long it takes individual learners to do a particular assignment.

We know that students have responsibilities and activities outside school, yet homework is often assigned at 3:00 p.m. one day and expected back the next day. We know that families differ in their priorities, yet many teachers believe all students should arrange their daily schedules to put homework first. These common practices reflect the old paradigm—how we *do* homework.

The beliefs and assumptions inherent in the old paradigm, coupled with the history of behaviorist practices in education, create a strange dynamic: when students fail to complete homework, we tend to approach the situation more like discipline than like learning. That is, remedies for students who don't do their homework tend to focus on punitive solutions as the key to changing behavior—consequences such as points off, failing grades, or missing recess or lunch to complete homework. We tend to get stuck in the reward/punishment box. Yet somehow, in our hearts, we know that we cannot *punish* students into completing homework.

Grading in the Old Paradigm

A primary method of reward and punishment for homework is grading. In fact, grading plays a huge role in the old homework paradigm. In an effort to force compliance, teachers give zeros for incomplete homework, and late policies mandate points off for each day homework is turned in late. Depending on what percentage homework counts for in the student's total grade, many *D*s and *F*s can result each semester from incomplete homework. The question arises: What do those *D*s and *F*s represent—a lack of learning or a lack of compliance?

Teachers often defend late policies by saying they are using them to teach responsibility. As discussed in Chapter 1, the teaching of responsibility is a much-touted goal, conjuring up images of compliant children dutifully toiling over whatever task was assigned to them (Kohn, 2006). Homework can play an important role in the development of that self-direction. However, those skills are not developed simply by assigning homework tasks and applying consequences if tasks are not completed (Kohn, 2006). The flaw in this concept lies in the implementation—when students don't complete homework on time, late policies punish them for *not learning* responsibility! So if they don't complete homework on time, doesn't that mean that the teacher has failed to *teach* them responsibility? If that is true, the logical act would be to *reteach* them without penalty. Instead, the use of late policies judges students for not learning responsibility and then fails them as a result. (Actually, unless responsibility is listed as a learning target in the academic curriculum, it shouldn't be assessed in the grade.)

What if all the students in our class failed to turn in homework on time? Would we fail everyone? Or do we only penalize some students for incomplete homework because we can compare the "good" students with the "bad" ones? Do late policies allow us to norm-reference our grades—and achieve a bell-shaped curve?

~~~~~~~~~~~~~~~~~~~~~~~~~~~~~~~~~~~~~

Homework 40, Football 0

In a high school in Texas, homework counted for up to 40 percent of the student's grade, depending on the subject. One year, even with tutoring from their coach, many members of the junior varsity football team were not keeping up with homework and were failing to make the minimum grades required to play sports. Primarily as a result of homework, the junior varsity football season had to be canceled one year.

Does this seem like a reasonable consequence? How would you prevent this situation from happening in the future?

As a solution to the problem, teachers decided to give less homework but make it count more in the grade. (Huh?)

~~~~~~~~~~~~~~~~~~~~~~~~~~~~~~~~~~~~~

As discussed in Chapter 2, when we use grades to punish late homework, we are often penalizing students for their home environment. It's not fair if students are punished because they have not had the opportunity to do the homework while at home. One student told her teacher, "My mother won't let me do homework." When questioned further, the student explained that she was required to cook, clean, and take care of younger siblings from the time she got home from school until bedtime. (Chapter 5 discusses a variety of solutions to this problem, other than failing grades.)

Although teachers often agree it is not fair to fail students because of homework, invariably someone will ask, "What about the less able student who actually passes *because* he or she has turned in homework?" That brings us to another grading dilemma. Homework should not cause children to fail, but should homework alone allow students to pass? Even if homework tasks reflect learning, it is difficult to be sure the student was the person who did the work. (Have you seen some of the incredible science fair projects from children of engineers?) Learning can be validly assessed only in the classroom or through external projects that have been closely monitored. Effort on homework alone should not equal a higher grade if the student cannot demonstrate knowledge of the content while in the classroom (Dueck,

2014; Guskey, 2003). Rewarding effort in the absence of learning is not a problem except when the reward is a grade, which is supposed to reflect learning. By allowing students to pass based on homework, we are still using grades to manipulate behavior, again rewarding compliance and not necessarily learning.

Rewarding homework compliance with good grades can result in two types of grade/learning mismatches. Sometimes, *high-achieving* students demonstrate mastery on assessments and class assignments but receive a *low grade* because of missing or late homework. Other times, *low-achieving* students show little mastery of the content but receive a *high grade* because they turn in all homework on time. In one school where homework counts heavily in student grades, the principal tells the story of a 7th grade girl who had received straight *A*s on her report card but whose parents were upset that she tested at a 4th grade reading level. Similarly, high school teachers have witnessed students with very high grades due to homework who could not earn decent scores on college entrance exams. In both cases, the students' homework compliance "saved" them, but a high grade without mastery is no gift (Vatterott, 2015).

Limitations of the Old Paradigm: Why It Doesn't Work

Inherent in the old paradigm are the assumptions that all students can do the work (not all of them can), that all students have the time to do the work (not all of them do), and that students should take as much time as is necessary to do the work (not all of them will). The old paradigm operates on the assumption that the child is capable of doing the work (Goldberg, 2012). When students are given homework that is beyond their comprehension level or that is too lengthy and are then penalized with failing grades for incorrect work, the experience is frustrating and demotivating (Vatterott, 2003, 2010). When those grades are permanent, there is no redemption for mistakes. Homework can also do harm when a student misunderstands a concept or a process (such as the steps in solving an equation) and homework causes the student to reinforce misconceptions or internalize bad habits.

For students who *can* do the homework and complete assignments on time, grading can be a positive experience. But for those students who struggle, the old homework paradigm leads to what Goldberg (2007, 2012) calls the "homework trap":

> Late work means points off, and work not done garners zeros. Their grades decline, setting into motion a number of actions by the parents and the school, with counteractions (usually inactions) by the children themselves. The problem is cumulative and colors the experiences these children have with school, affecting their attitudes and performance in later years. (Goldberg, 2007, p. 1)

After a while, failing grades from incomplete homework accumulate and are almost impossible to counteract. This can lead to a feeling of helplessness—why bother to even try to catch up? The homework trap activates the following chain reaction:

> Incomplete homework→poor grades→poor attitudes→a predictable avoidance of homework and a resentment toward the system→more failing grades. (adapted from Goldberg, 2007, p. 2)

What the homework trap shows us is the importance of the emotional dynamic of the assessment experience (Stiggins, 2007; Vatterott, 2015). Motivation and a sense of competence are key factors in student success (Horsley & Walker, 2013). Because grading is perceived by students as judging, it separates students into winners and losers. It is precisely the practice of punishing noncompliance regarding homework that interferes with the effective practice of homework, to the detriment of learning and motivation.

The goal of assessment of learning should be to keep failure at bay and to maintain the learner's confidence—the opposite of what occurs in the homework trap. The most important question to ask about the grading of homework is "What is the effect on future learning?" (Goldberg, 2012; Stiggins, 2007). Priority must be given to tasks that do not cause students to give up.

What is the result of not being a successful player in the homework game? Motivation to learn may be affected as well as learner identity. Students on a "losing streak" feel hopeless. They begin to think, "This hurts. I'm not safe here; I just can't do this . . . again. I'm confused. I don't like this—help! Nothing I try seems to work" (Stiggins, 2007, p. 24). In such situations, homework can actually discourage some students from further learning. To protect their self-esteem and reputation, these students often adopt a cover; they claim they don't do homework because they "just don't want to" rather than admitting they don't understand the assignment or don't have the time or the proper conditions to do homework (Vatterott, 2014).

Luis's Story

Luis was failing social studies because he was missing 11 assignments. When the teacher's aide tried to find out why, Luis said, "I'm lazy." In fact, Luis felt hopelessly buried in work. The teacher's aide volunteered to stay after school to help Luis catch up. It was hard convincing Luis to stay after school, but after several work sessions, he was caught up and no longer called himself lazy.

The homework trap explains why some students don't do homework. The trap shows how we set them up for failure and why they give up. Often, the result is students who simply refuse to do homework. The old paradigm gives students that option—students who do not complete homework are given failing grades but are not required to complete the work. Not only does this cause students to receive failing grades, but it also puts some students at a disadvantage. If the homework they are not doing is quality homework, a gap in skills and confidence may arise between students who regularly complete homework and those who do not, often exacerbating the achievement gap.

Simply stated, the old paradigm short-circuits our long-term goals by allowing students to fail by not doing homework. It creates practical and motivational obstacles that converge to form the perfect storm for student failure. Traditional practices can discourage the very quality we are trying to instill: accountability. "We are faced with the irony that a policy that may be grounded in the belief of holding students accountable (giving zeros) actually allows some students to escape accountability for *learning*" (emphasis added) (O'Connor, 2007, p. 86).

The old paradigm was about accountability for *working*, not *learning*. But today our long-term goals go beyond compliance with authority. Our long-term goals are for students to develop and use higher-order thinking skills and to be confident, independent learners. When some students don't do homework (quality homework, that is), those long-term goals may be compromised.

Our goal is to develop and refine students' intellectual skills—but when students don't do homework, they may not perfect their math skills or read as well, and they may lack depth of knowledge for future learning.

Our goal is to develop confident, independent learners—but when students don't do homework, they may fail to develop strategies for independent work and miss the sense of efficacy that comes from completing tasks on their own.

The effect of homework grades may also be negative. First, if incomplete homework produces poor results on course assessments, lower grades may result. Second, when incomplete homework is counted as a zero in the total average, students receive lower grades for the semester or the year. In some cases, these lower grades may cause students to fail subjects in elementary school or courses in middle school or high school. At the elementary and middle school levels, failure in more than one subject may be grounds for retention. For high school students, failing semester grades affect grade point average, which again influences their access to college.

Getting Homework Right: Creating a New Paradigm for Homework

To reach our long-term goals as well as to meet short-term academic purposes, it is necessary to create a new homework paradigm that focuses on academic success for all students. Creating such a paradigm requires a comprehensive set of practices that can improve academic success when implemented as a package. These practices are the following:

- Designing quality homework tasks
- Differentiating homework tasks
- Moving from grading to checking
- Deemphasizing the grading of homework
- Using completion strategies
- Establishing homework support programs

Completion strategies and homework support programs are discussed in Chapter 5.

Before addressing the first of these (designing quality homework tasks), we must consider the purpose of the homework task and how it relates to what is learned in the classroom.

What Is the Purpose of the Homework Task?

Since the first edition of this book, my thoughts on the purpose of homework have evolved. In standards-based learning, our goal is for all students to reach the standards; Figure 4.1 outlines that shift in purpose. The five purposes listed in the right-hand column are consistent with that goal.

FIGURE 4.1
The Shift in the Purpose of Homework

Marzano, Pickering, and Pollock (2001)	Vatterott (2009)	Vatterott (2018)
• Preparation • Practice • Extension	• Prelearning • Checking for understanding • Practice • Processing	• Prelearning • Diagnosis • Checking for understanding • Practice at the application level • Processing (*reflection, application, analysis, synthesis*)

Prelearning. Traditional preparatory homework, such as reading or outlining a chapter before a discussion, was often used to introduce a topic or provide background for a more in-depth lesson. In the worst-case scenario, prelearning consisted of new learning that students were expected to master on their own, ahead of the lesson—an inefficient use of homework.

Rather than dictating what students read or outline, a more engaging use of prelearning would be to discover what students already know about a topic or what they are interested in learning about—for example, asking them to write down questions they have about the digestive system. The most valuable use of prelearning homework may be to stimulate interest in a concept (e.g., having students list the eye color and hair color of relatives for a genetics lesson). One strategy to spark student interest in an upcoming lesson is an entry slip with a question for students to explore. Figure 4.2 shows a sample entry slip that allows students to read anything they choose about the question and asks them to respond to three of the four prompts.

Diagnosis. How can we design standards-based learning if we don't know where students are? Diagnostic homework helps answer the question *Where do I start?*, providing information that

---

FIGURE 4.2
Sample Entry Slip

Directions:

The point of the reading/research is not to *definitively answer* the question, but to *explore and reflect on* the question.

1. What you read is your choice. For example, you may read any textbook excerpts, articles, blog posts, or educational websites or conduct an Internet search seeking information about the question.
2. Answer at least three of the four prompts below.
3. Bring your entry slip to class on the day the question is listed.

Today's research question: *Why was the Vietnam War controversial?*
What I read: _____

Prompts:

 Something I learned from what I read that **squared** with my thinking or beliefs:

 Something I saw from a new **angle**—an "aha" moment or a surprise:

 Ideas that are still **circling** in my head (not sure about *or* yes, but . . .):

 Another question the research question made me think of:

---

enables the teacher to make decisions about next steps (Depka, 2015). Diagnostic homework might include a KWL chart, a pretest, a checklist of "I can" statements (Schimmer, 2012), or a practice test to assess prior knowledge (e.g., 4th, 5th, and 6th grade–level questions for 6th graders). Diagnostic homework both shapes instruction for all and guides individual learning. It also saves time: once teachers know where students are in their skills or knowledge, they can plan instruction more efficiently. Jeff Harding, a math teacher at Mundelein High School in Mundelein, Illinois, calls his pre-tests of prerequisite skills "mastery checks." He uses the results to design refresher tasks and learning targets for the course (Vatterott, 2015).

Checking for understanding. Checking for understanding is probably the most neglected use of homework, yet it is the most valuable way for teachers to gain insight into student learning. For instance, journal questions about a science experiment may ask the student to explain what happened and why. Asking students to identify literary devices in a short story shows the teacher whether the student understands literary devices. Asking students to do a few sample problems in math and to explain the steps lets the teacher know if the student understands how to do the problem. In Eva Rudolph's math class at Fox Middle School in Arnold, Missouri, homework is creating a "proof" for such learning targets as "I can use properties to write equivalent equations," enabling Eva to quickly check for understanding.

Practice. The traditional use of homework has been for the practice of rote skills, such as multiplication tables, or things that need to be memorized, such as spelling words. Although practice is necessary for many rote skills, there are three mistakes that teachers sometimes make with the use of practice homework. First, teachers may believe they are giving practice homework when, in fact, the student did not understand the concept or skill in class. The homework then actually involves new learning and is often quite frustrating. Second, if teachers skip the step of checking for understanding, students may be practicing something incorrectly and internalizing misconceptions. For instance, students should practice math operations only *after* the teacher has adequately checked for understanding. Third, distributed practice is better than mass practice—that is, practice is more effective when distributed over several days (Hattie & Yates, 2014; Willingham & Daniel, 2012). In other words, a student may need to practice a math operation 50 times to master it, but not all in one night! A common practice for math teachers today is to give two-tiered math homework: for example, Part One is 3 problems to check for understanding of a new concept, and Part Two is 10 problems to practice a concept previously learned.

Processing. Processing homework is used when we want students to reflect on concepts that were discussed in class, think of new questions to ask, apply skills or knowledge learned, synthesize information, or show that they see the big picture. Processing homework is often a long-term project, such as showing relationships between major concepts in a unit, writing an original poem, or applying a number of math concepts to the design of a golf course.

Designing Quality Homework Tasks

Understanding the purpose of homework will not, by itself, ensure that students will be motivated to complete homework tasks. Although motivation is complex and unique to individuals, teachers can increase the likelihood that homework will be completed by considering the needs of the individual learner in the design of the homework task itself. Designing quality homework tasks requires attention to four aspects, each of which affects students' motivation to approach the task and their perseverance in completing it:

- *Academic purpose*—Tasks should have a clear academic purpose.
- *Efficiency*—Tasks should help students reach the standard without wasting time or energy.
- *Competence*—Tasks should have a positive effect on a student's sense of competence.
- *Ownership*—Tasks should be personally relevant and customized to promote ownership (Vatterott, 2010).

Academic Purpose

Students often do not complete homework simply because the task is not meaningful. The most egregious homework practice is to assign busywork or tasks of dubious academic value that do not reinforce existing knowledge or demonstrate a mastery of knowledge (Cushman, 2010b; Past, 2006; Pope, 2010; Vatterott, 2010). Sometimes busywork is born from the attitudes discussed in Chapter 1—that homework must be assigned regardless of the value of the task. Sometimes homework tasks are well-intentioned attempts to have students do something fun or interesting, but the academic focus is not apparent. (What, exactly, is the learning purpose of a word search or a diorama? What evidence of learning do those tasks show?) Writing out definitions of vocabulary words, taking notes while reading a novel, or coloring in a map may sound like good homework, but one might question whether those tasks are appropriate when today's academic standards focus on higher-order thinking.

Standards-based learning has raised the bar: rote practice is out; task complexity is in. After all, low-level rote practice is meaningless without context. To facilitate higher-level learning, students should practice skills not in isolation, but through appli-cation. *Application* of rote skills or facts compels practice and deepens understanding. No one ever said Bloom's taxonomy had to be a *linear* process. When tasks have clear academic purpose, students don't just write spelling words; they use them to write declarative essays. They don't define the parts of the cell; they create an analogy for the cell parts and functions. They don't complete 20 identical math problems; they apply math skills to new problems (Vatterott, 2015). Instead of asking students to keep *reading logs,* which simply document that students (or parents) read, a better task would be to have students write a *reading blog* to discuss what they have been reading. Tasks requiring rote memory must be thought through carefully, given the access to rote knowledge that is available today. How much memorization do we really need in today's world? If students can Google it, do they really need to memorize it?

The ultimate goal of the assignment—prelearning, diagnosis, checking for understanding, practice, or processing—as well as its connection to classroom learning should be explicitly communicated to students (Brookhart, 2017; Depka, 2015). Ideally, all homework should show the learning target for that task (Vatterott, 2015). If not, teachers can create purpose statements for homework tasks that may be explained orally or written on the homework sheet itself. Some sample statements are shown in Figure 4.3.

FIGURE 4.3
Sample Purpose Statements for Homework

For Younger Students
The reason for today's homework is . . .
- So you can practice doing something you learned in school.
- So I can find out if you understand what you learned today.
- So you can think about and write about what you learned.
- So you can tell me what you think about what you learned.
- To show you something we will learn about soon.
- To help you get ready to take a test or quiz.

For Older Students
The reason for today's homework is to . . .
- Allow you to practice something you have already learned.
- Allow you to apply something you have already learned to a new situation.
- Check whether you understand something you have already learned.
- Allow you to analyze something you have already learned.
- Allow you to pull together several things that you have already learned.
- Allow you to reflect on your learning.

Efficiency

Some traditional homework tasks may be *inefficient*, either because they show no evidence of learning or because they take an inordinate amount of time. Projects that require nonacademic skills like cutting, gluing, or drawing are often inefficient. Classic projects like dioramas, models, and poster displays are created by teachers who see them as a fun, creative way for students to show what they have learned. But unless content requirements are clearly spelled out in a rubric, projects often reveal much less about students' content knowledge than about their artistic talents. Even content-rich tasks such as lengthy research papers can be inefficient in terms of time spent. Is it necessary to read the *whole* book? Does the research paper really need to be 10 pages long? Often, teachers don't realize how many hours students spend on an assignment or how tedious it may be for both students and parents.

For many types of projects, there are more efficient ways to accomplish the same goal and to better demonstrate student learning. Instead of creating a diorama of life during the Reconstruction, students could write a diary entry as if they were living in the time, discussing daily life, race relations, and laws that affect them. Instead of building a model of the solar system, students could create a chart to show the planets' temperature extremes and periods of rotation in Earth time, and the importance of inertia and gravity to the motion of the planets (Vatterott, 2010).

Competence

One of the goals of homework is to ensure that students will feel positive about learning and develop an identity as successful learners. Homework tasks should be designed not only to support classroom learning but also to instill a sense of competence in the mind of the learner (Lin-Siegler et al., 2016). In fact, when students feel unsuccessful in approaching homework tasks, they often avoid the tasks completely as a way to protect their self-esteem. A major problem with homework is the demotivating effect of tasks that students are unable to complete on their own (Darling-Hammond & Ifill-Lynch, 2006; Goldberg, 2012; Vatterott, 2010). Homework that cannot be done without help is not good homework.

Failure-oriented students are particularly sensitive about how they feel about approaching a task. If certain tasks reinforce their view of themselves as "smarter," they will more likely attempt those tasks (Dweck, 2007; Vatterott, 2015). Being successful at completing homework feeds students' sense of competence. They will avoid tasks that make them feel "dumber" to protect their self-esteem. "I didn't do it because it was a stupid assignment" often means "I couldn't do it, so it made me feel stupid" (Vatterott, 2014). This avoidance tendency means that for struggling students, hard tasks should come later, after they have accomplished easier tasks and feel confident in approaching homework. Poor grades on homework contribute to "feeling judged" and to a sense of failure, which increases anxiety and often causes students to avoid tasks they may be capable of successfully completing (Goldberg, 2012). (The effects of grading are discussed at greater length later in the chapter.)

Just as checking for understanding is an important purpose for homework, teachers also need to check for frustration. Some will say frustration is good for students—that they must learn to work through it, that it builds character. But how much frustration is too much? At some point, students will shut down and refuse to work. Teachers should solicit feedback from students, finding out how students feel about approaching certain tasks and how they feel after they've attempted those tasks. When homework is not completed, teachers should talk with students to find out why. (Tools and methods to assist teachers in gathering this information are discussed in Chapter 5.)

Ownership

Often, when students will not do homework, we fail to examine the learning task we have given them. Instead of asking, "How do we get them to do their homework?" we should be asking, "What's the task?" (Cushman, 2010a; Darling-Hammond & Ifill-Lynch, 2006; Kohn, 2006). Students are often unmotivated to do homework because they do not perceive it as important. It's just a task to do with no personal relevance or individuality.

What's wrong with this picture? In many classrooms, students feel little or no ownership of their learning in general—we teach, we assign tasks, we test, and students are the passive receptacles (Wiliam, 2016). They have no stake in the outcome— it doesn't mean anything to them—because it's not about them. As long as learning and homework are being "done to" them, the goals are ours, not theirs (Kohn, 2006). As a teacher once said, "I've never heard of a child not doing *his* work; it's *our* work he's not doing" (Vatterott, 2015).

Think about all the imperfections we accept from very young children as they learn skills like feeding and dressing themselves. We instinctively realize that messy high chairs and snow boots worn in summer are less important than mastery of the skill and the pride that comes with it. We fully understand the freedom that is required for children to take ownership of those tasks. Yet when it comes to academic learning, we often fail to appreciate the innate desire for mastery or trust the child's knowledge of how to get there. So we assign a single task as homework and expect all students to comply. And *voilà!* Learning occurs. Except when it doesn't (Vatterott, 2014).

If we claim that we want students to take responsibility for homework, we must give them more control over what they learn, how they learn it, and how they show that they've learned it (Guskey & Anderman, 2008). We must move away from one-size-fits-all, teacher-dictated tasks to involve students in the design of their own learning. What drives learning is *not* rewards and punishments, points and zeros, but students' sense of mastery, autonomy, and purpose (Azzam, 2014; Pink, 2009). "Intrinsic motivation flows from ownership" (Anderson, 2016, p. 16).

Like those milestones in early childhood development, student ownership of homework is not perfect, but it is powerful. When students know themselves as learners and how they best learn, and when they are free to connect personally with the content, learning becomes joyful and intrinsically rewarding and need not be incentivized.

How is student ownership of homework achieved? It starts with choice (Anderson, 2016). Homework choice can be as limited as asking students to "pick any 10 of these 30 problems to solve," as specific as having students work only on learning targets that they are struggling with, or as wide open as a self-selected, self-designed project. Students may not have a choice about the learning goal, but they can almost always be given a choice as to the path they take to reach the goal.

For instance, suppose the learning goal for all students is to memorize their multiplication tables. The homework might look like this:

1. Create your own method to memorize your multiplication tables. Some ideas other students have tried include reciting, making note cards, drawing a grid or a color-coded chart, or creating a rap song.
2. Share your idea with the class tomorrow.
3. Practice your method this week.
4. Evaluate how well your method worked after the no-count quiz on Friday.

Flipped Homework

A relatively recent innovation that attends to all four aspects of designing quality homework tasks is *flipped homework,* or flipped learning. Flipped homework is the practice of delivering direct instruction and basic content to students through an instructional video as homework and then spending class time on application, analysis, and practice (Bergmann, 2017). Flipped homework is becoming increasingly popular, especially in more affluent communities where teachers are confident that all students have Internet access. Flipped learning has grown from an instructional model into a movement that is transforming education around the world. The Flipped Learning Global Initiative (www.flglobal.org) is a worldwide coalition of educators who support research, training, and implementation of flipped learning.

Flipped homework has the potential not only to make homework more efficient and purposeful but also to allow for student ownership and competence. In a survey of more than 2,000 K–12 students currently experiencing flipped homework, 52 percent reported that it took less time than traditional homework, and 67 percent reported that the videos made understanding the content "easier" or "much easier" (Bergmann, 2017, pp. 23–29). This is not surprising, since videos allow students to pause, rewind, and repeat instruction as needed. Flipping can be made even more efficient by asking students to go beyond watching the video and taking notes. Some teachers ask students to complete a formative assessment about the video and rate their level of understanding, which is used the next day to group students for follow-up tasks.

Differentiating Homework Tasks

Differentiating homework tasks allows the teacher to meet the individual needs of students. Students who have been successful learners need to continue with increasingly challenging material and to maintain the confidence to learn new concepts and skills. Students who master concepts quickly may need to be assigned more independent work or extended research. Students with severe disabilities must be given tasks at which they can be successful so that they will persevere. Equally at risk, English language learners (ELLs) must be allowed to experience success in their native language until they are able to learn in English (Chappuis, 2014). In addition, students with learning difficulties must be convinced that they can be capable learners and that their deficits can be remediated with hard work (Vatterott, 2007). This academic remediation is essential to these students' continued engagement in school.

How can homework be differentiated? To meet the needs of a variety of learners, most teachers differentiate homework in one of three ways: by difficulty or amount of work, by the amount of structure or scaffolding provided, or by learning preference or interest.

Differentiating by Difficulty or Amount of Work

Homework tasks that are too difficult for students to complete are a major demotivator for many students, especially academically challenged students (Tomlinson, 2014a; Vatterott, 2010). To keep students motivated and willing to approach homework, tasks must be differentiated by level of difficulty (Anderson, 2016). Students differ in their ability to understand concepts or in their skill level with particular tasks. Diagnosing and determining that readiness helps teachers answer this question: What level of work can the student successfully complete? This may be determined through pre-tests, by observation of the students' understanding during class, or from their performance on previous homework.

Students with limited readiness may need homework involving simpler reading material or tasks that are more concrete. Instead of reading the textbooks, some students may use adapted reading packets that come with the text, which outline the main ideas of each chapter. More advanced students may benefit from more challenging tasks or the opportunity to explore topics in greater depth (Tomlinson, 2014a).

For example, in one teacher's high school physical science class, a homework assignment involved eight questions to demonstrate understanding of kinetic and potential energy. All students were expected to complete those questions. A challenge question was also given. All students were encouraged to attempt the challenge question, but only the students taking geometry were *required* to. The teacher explains: "I expect all kids to at least attempt the challenge problems, to show what formula to use. But as far as manipulating the math, I don't expect a pre-algebra kid to be able to do that math. It's multiple steps with harder vocabulary."

Closely related to difficulty, and equally important, is the *amount* of work students are assigned. On the one hand, the same task that takes the average student 15 minutes to complete could take another student more than an hour, causing some students to spend excessive time on homework. On the other hand, students who quickly and easily master concepts may become frustrated if asked to complete the same number of practice problems as students who have not yet mastered a concept. A simple means of differentiation is to ask all students to complete what work they can in a specific amount of time: "Do what you can in 20 minutes; draw a line, and work longer if you like." This approach provides valuable feedback to the teacher about working speed and level of understanding. When teachers make clear to students how long a task *should* take, it helps students evaluate their own learning. The conversation might go something like this: "If it's taking you more than 20 minutes to get it done, that's a red flag. You didn't pay attention or you don't have the notes—there's something wrong. No homework assignment in my class should take longer than 20 minutes."

Many elementary teachers use the 10-minute rule to differentiate for students. One teacher's policy for her 5th graders' homework is "50 minutes is 50 minutes." Students are not expected to work more than 50 minutes each night. If students have homework in math, science, and reading and they spend 50 minutes on science and math, parents simply write a note saying, "We spent our 50 minutes on science and math and had no time for reading tonight." When homework for multiple subjects is given on the same night, teachers can easily specify which subjects should be prioritized if the student does not have adequate time.

Decisions about how many problems to assign or how many pages to read must consider the student's working speed as well as motivation and persistence. Because academically challenged learners are easily discouraged, care must be taken to limit the amount of work to what the student can complete in a reasonable amount of time.

Many teachers have discovered that the rate of homework completion skyrockets when they simply give less work. Most students are eager to be successful when the difficulty and amount of work are reasonable.

Which brings us to a dilemma. How do we find more time for learners who need it? Often, teachers expect learners with a slower working speed to simply spend more time on homework than other students. The quandary is that these learners usually are less persistent, tire more quickly, and often have less resilience with academic tasks. Like everyone, they need downtime. With only so much time in a day, it seems unfair for them to have to work longer. When differentiating for learners who work more slowly, the first questions teachers should ask are these: Have we accurately diagnosed the student's readiness and learning strengths? Should learning targets be prioritized to fewer more essential goals? Is our feedback about learning moving the student forward? These questions lead us to two other methods of differentiating homework: providing structure or scaffolding and differentiating by learning preference or interest.

Differentiating by Amount of Structure or Scaffolding

Adding structure to homework tasks may help some students, especially struggling students and ELLs. Providing structure or scaffolding can help students feel the job is within their capabilities and can be completed without frustration. One of the simplest ways to help students is to require less writing, giving them assignments with fewer blanks to fill in or with answers that can be circled instead of written out. Many struggling students have poor fine-motor skills, which makes writing tedious.

Some students may be expected to create a graphic organizer of their reading, and others may be provided with the skeleton of an organizer and be required to fill in only a few key ideas. Some students may be given a word bank for answering questions or a copy of class notes to help them study. Class notes may be provided by the teacher or by another student. Math homework may be given with a choice of correct answers, or math manipulatives may be loaned out for homework. Teachers may allow some students to use a peer helper whom they can call if they have problems with homework. Hint sheets or lists of supplemental websites can also be given.

For some students, cursive writing makes assignments more difficult. Developmentally delayed elementary students and ELL students often struggle with cursive writing. Directions for homework may be printed instead of given in cursive writing, and students may be allowed to print or type content assignments.

ELL students may benefit from assignments with pictures and may find it easier to complete assignments in their native language first. Those assignments can be translated later by the student, using an app or a pocket translator or enlisting the help of a bilingual peer or teacher. This approach allows the student to concentrate on one skill at a time. Similarly, when learning a multistep math process, students with limited readiness may need to master steps one at a time instead of attempting to learn the entire process at once.

Differentiating by Learning Preference or Interest

As discussed earlier, students enjoy choices and the ability to express their individuality. Adapting homework assignments to students' learning preferences or interests is a quick path to fostering a sense of ownership of the homework task.

One of the easiest ways to capitalize on learning preferences is to allow students to choose which method they will use to demonstrate what they have learned. Students may write, type, audio-record, or use pictures. Students may also decide on the best way for them to practice rote memory tasks (such as the multiplication table example given earlier). Instead of all students writing spelling words three times, students could be asked to design their own method for memorizing the words. Some may do it orally, some by typing or writing, others by tracing the letters with their finger. Tactile learners may benefit from cards with raised images made from sandpaper-like material to learn such concepts as letters, geometric shapes, or geographic features. Figure 4.4 shows examples of how homework can be differentiated.

Personalized homework. The ultimate way to differentiate homework for student interest is to use *personalized homework,* which involves students in setting goals, planning a specific home-work task, and determining how they will demonstrate learning. Personalized homework is an extension of the *personalized learn-ing* movement, which capitalizes on student interests and taps into students' intrinsic need to control their own learning.

Personalized learning is an umbrella term used to describe a variety of student-centered options typically involving student goal setting, inquiry, and design of learning. It may refer to an all-encompassing learning system with customized academic pathways for individual students; a technology-based, self-paced learning system; or an occasional independent project. As Kallick and Zmuda (2017) describe it,

> In personalized learning, students work with the teacher to develop a challenge, problem, or idea; to clarify what is being measured (learning goals); to envision the product or performance (assessment); and to outline an action plan that will result in an outcome that achieves the desired results (learning actions). (pp. 3–4)

FIGURE 4.4
What Differentiated Homework Looks Like

Purpose of Homework	Example of Skill or Content	Differentiation for Difficulty/ Amount of Work	Differentiation for Scaffolding/ Structure	Differentiation for Learning Preference/Interest
Practice of rote memory	Multiplication tables	Some students may work on only one set at a time until they achieve some mastery. Other students may work on several sets at one time.	Some students may have a completed grid that they trace. Some students may write from memory.	Students may choose to write, recite, create their own table, or set tables to music to help them learn.
Practice of a skill	Division of whole numbers	Some students' problems will use two-digit numbers, some three-digit numbers, some four-digit numbers. Some students will be assigned fewer problems.	Some students will receive problems that are partially filled in—they provide the missing numbers. Some students will have explanations of steps written in the margin of their assignment.	Students may write and solve their own word problems, or they may complete practice problems from one of several math websites.
Prelearning	Main ideas of the chapter	Some students will have abbreviated reading assignments focusing only on certain sections of chapter. Some will have focused questions to guide them to main ideas.	Some students may be given an advance organizer. Some may have a word bank to choose main ideas from.	Students may draw a graphic summary of the main ideas and list the three most interesting things about the chapter.
Checking for understanding	Causes and effects of the Boston Tea Party	Some students will read the textbook. Other students may read a simpler version written as a play.	Some students will list the causes and effects of the Boston Tea Party. Other students will receive a list with some causes or some effects provided and have to fill in the blanks.	Students may defend or criticize the actions of the participants of the Boston Tea Party with an editorial, a poster, or a concept map.

The personalized homework that's probably most familiar to teachers is *genius hour* (also called *passion projects*): giving students a block of time to learn more about something that they are curious about or that excites or inspires them. These long-term projects often start in the classroom and then transition to homework, with students bringing them back periodically for feedback and eventually presenting their results to an audience. Cryslynn Billingsley's 7th graders spend one hour in class each week on their genius hour projects (with monthly goals), but most of the work is done at home. Each May, students proudly present their projects at the Genius Hour Showcase. Parents and community members are invited to see the projects and learn more from the students themselves (Billingsley, 2014). Student projects have focused on such diverse topics as animal rights, effects of the media, and how the brain learns. Parents have been astonished by the sophistication of the students' research.

Personalized homework such as this provides high-interest opportunities for students to apply critical thinking skills and sparks their enthusiasm for future learning. The motivational value of personalized homework cannot be overstated. As a result, teachers at all levels are experimenting with giving students the freedom to learn more about their passions.

"Sounds great," you may say, "but I have to teach to the standards." It's true that most teachers are still required to teach to standards and are held accountable for how well their students are reaching those standards. And no, it may not be feasible for *all* homework to be personalized. But consider this: if the mandated curriculum is so unappealing that students are not engaged or completing homework anyway, could personalized homework reignite their interest in learning?

An additional challenge for teachers is the perceived loss of control. The decision to use personalized homework *at all* is a function of how much control teachers are comfortable giving up. It may be helpful to think of the amount of ownership students are given and the amount of control teachers relinquish as degrees on a continuum. Traditional homework is designed by teachers with no student input or choice; teachers have total control. Letting go of that control can be scary! As we grant students more ownership, we may offer choices, or we may differentiate. To give students ultimate ownership, we may allow them to pursue personalized paths, giving up a lot of control! Figure 4.5 illustrates this continuum.

FIGURE 4.5
Continuum of Student Ownership of Homework

Teacher Ownership		Student Ownership
Traditional *No student control*	**Differentiated** *Some student control*	**Personalized** *Significant student control*
• One-size-fits-all • Teacher-prescribed	• Choices driven by standard and/or specific student need • Teacher- or student-prescribed	• Choices driven by student interest (e.g., genius hour) • Student-designed
No student voice or choice	Some student voice and choice	Significant student voice and choice

Is there a middle ground between no student control and almost total student control of homework? Absolutely. Suppose the standards that individual students are struggling with *could* be reached through personalized, student-directed homework. At Vinal Elementary School in Norwell, Massachusetts, teachers are doing just that with standards-based learning that blends personalized homework with teacher-guided tasks. Students start by identifying their learning preferences and pinpointing their strengths and weaknesses, looking through their portfolios to determine where they need improvement. Then students, parents, and teachers work together to set measurable goals aligned to learning standards. Homework is used as a tool to meet those goals. Students set personal goals related to the standards and practice the skills they need to work on, but they are given choices of tasks and may apply the skill or concept to an area of personal interest. All students are working toward the same standards, and for the most part it's the students who are creating the homework tasks, with some teacher input. One of Robin Thibodeau's 2nd graders saw trophies at her brother's tae kwon do class, decided to count them to practice her addition and subtraction, and wrote word problems about them for her homework. Kelli Meade's 4th graders apply learning standards to their individual interests, develop an action plan, and present their research about such topics as the science of flight, snakes, and 3-D structures (Vatterott, 2017).

Standards, curriculum, the unique needs of students, and teacher comfort level are all factors that must be weighed as teachers decide whether personalized homework is desirable for their students. As Rebora (2017) notes, "There are legitimate questions of balance and degree when it comes to personalization. How much independent, personally oriented learning is really constructive for students? At what point do you jeopardize content knowledge or lose important aspects of a common curriculum?" (p. 7).

What makes sense for many teachers is a balance of choice, differentiated homework, and personalized homework over the course of a semester or year. Often, some personalized homework will be blended into day-to-day learning in tandem with other, more teacher-directed assignments. Many teachers reserve personalized homework for times when student motivation wanes, such as before winter break or near the end of the school year.

Moving from Grading to Checking: Focusing on Feedback

As discussed in Chapter 3, research has shown feedback to be more powerful than many other factors that influence learning (Hattie, 2009, 2012). The purpose of homework should be to provide feedback to the teacher and the student about how learning is progressing. The purpose is all about what informs learning and what informs the teacher. As we move into the feedback mode, we use completed assignments to revise future assignments. Feedback that revises instruction is often missing in the old homework paradigm. This omission is why the new paradigm changes the role of grading (Vatterott, 2015).

Grades are not necessary for learning to take place. In fact, research indicates that grades tend to interfere with learning (Guskey, 2003; Kohn, 2011; O'Connor, 2013). Grades on homework often get in the way of learning, demotivate students, and create power struggles between students and teachers and between students and parents. When homework receives permanent grades, mistakes are inevitably penalized—which sends the harmful message that learning should be an error-free process. Grading is viewed as *evaluative* by students, who perceive the teacher as a judge (Guskey & Jung, 2013). By contrast, checking (providing ungraded feedback) is *diagnostic*—the teacher is working as an advocate for the student. Should all homework be graded? No. Should all homework receive feedback? Yes.

When teachers stop grading homework, many of them see an attitudinal shift—students come to trust that teachers are working together with them to meet their learning needs, and they feel a sense of empowerment and ownership over their own learning (Popham, 2008). Once the threat of grades is taken away from the homework experience, "homework becomes a safe place to try out new skills without penalty, just as athletes and musicians try out their skills on the practice field or in rehearsals" (Christopher, 2007–2008, p. 74).

Feedback as Formative Assessment *for* Learning

Homework's role should be as formative assessment—assessment *for* learning that takes place *during* learning (Brookhart, 2017). Homework's role is not assessment *of* learning; therefore, it should not be graded. As a teacher who was also a coach once said about homework, "We don't keep score during practice."

For many teachers, providing feedback without grades is a new way of communicating progress. They've never done homework without grades, and grades are the only way they know to give feedback. Letters and numbers are easy and fast, and they make up a language everyone *thinks* they understand. But there's a whole network of communication that many teachers are unaccustomed to using. Good feedback on homework requires back-and-forth dialogue between the teacher and the student. Homework gives the teacher feedback about student learning, which allows the teacher to adjust instruction and to give targeted feedback to the learner—and the cycle continues. Feedback is an "ongoing exchange between a teacher and his or her students" (Tomlinson, 2014b, p. 11).

Let's clarify the use of the term *formative assessment*. The term *formative assessment* is used generally to describe any method of giving feedback to students about their learning when there is still time to improve. Giving feedback about homework, checking homework for understanding, and helping students correct mistakes *is* formative assessment, even though many teachers just see these practices as good teaching. In our data-driven culture, the term *assessment* has been so drilled into our heads as being a *task* or a *test* that many teachers define formative assessment solely as teacher-designed tasks whose results are marked or documented so that students and parents have a record of the student's progress toward the learning targets. But feedback about homework often occurs more informally as an alternative to traditional grading.

The goal of feedback on homework is to improve learning, to improve performance on summative assessments, to promote student ownership of learning, and to encourage self-assessment (Brookhart, 2017). "When homework is used as a formative assessment, students have multiple opportunities to practice, get feedback from the teacher, and improve" (Christopher, 2007–2008, p. 74). "Good formative assessment gives students information they need to understand where they are in their learning (the cognitive factor) and develops students' feelings of control over their learning (the motivational factor)" (Brookhart, 2007–2008, p. 54).

Focusing on feedback to improve learning requires downsizing. Education consultant and author Grant Wiggins once said, "Teachers spend too much time teaching." Concerned about covering a glutted curriculum, teachers often become too focused on coverage to assess what students are actually mastering. Downsizing requires teachers to have clear goals, to prioritize concepts and skills for mastery, and to pare down content to a manageable amount. Focusing on feedback requires teachers to slow down—to teach less, assess more, and make time for reteaching some students or providing other students with additional assistance.

Efficient Ways of Providing Feedback

Busy teachers need quick and efficient methods of checking for understanding—even if those methods are less than perfect. High school science teacher Laura Eberle explains her process:

> I take 30 to 40 seconds to glance down, I see if it's complete, and I glance at their answers a bit. It doesn't take that long to get a general idea of where their hang-ups are. I do use [homework] as feedback for myself and what are they getting and what they are not.

Teachers who provide feedback efficiently often use their subjective judgment. One strategy is to do a quick visual check of homework each morning while students are working on another task. The teacher scans each assignment and puts the papers into two piles—students who appear to have understood the concept and students who didn't. Without marking papers, the teacher knows how to regroup students, reteach, or assign students to buddy pairs to go over concepts again. One 3rd grade teacher explains his procedure:

> Other teachers say, "How do you do that? It takes so much time." It takes less than five minutes a day to correct homework because I'm not "*correcting* homework." I'm looking at it to see if they did a good job, if they understood. Then I know I've got to meet with these three kids because they did not get last night's concept.

Teachers are not the only ones who can provide feedback. Feedback can also be given from student to student. Often, teachers will simply ask students to meet in groups to compare their homework answers, ask one another questions, and then report back to the teacher. The group discussions are often quite valuable; the back-and-forth conversation helps students clarify the goals of the assignment.

In Eva Rudolph's math class, students score their own homework, which must show their process as well as the answer. Then they meet in teams of four. The group must "verify" each student's self-scoring and "sign off" on it. If students can't reach consensus, they discuss why the work is not complete. The group then selects a few problems that it wants the teacher to review on the board.

In addition to peer assessment, self-assessment is often more efficient than when teachers assess learning. After all, who knows the student's level of understanding better than the student? Read on.

Helping Students Self-Assess

The ultimate realization of ownership comes when students assess their own learning. Yet this is easier said than done. Many students don't know how to self-assess because assessment has always been "done to" them. If they've been trained in a system of rote learning to just spit content back, then reflecting on and evaluating their own learning is a foreign concept to them (Guskey & Anderman, 2008; Vatterott, 2015). They need to be taught how, and they need to be given practice in the classroom.

Teachers can begin by asking students to rate how well they understood a homework assignment. This rating allows students to reflect on the homework task and to provide information to the teacher. Students can use one of three symbols or stickers at the top of the homework assignment to indicate their level of understanding:

Got it/understood	!/happy face/green sticker
Sort of got it/not sure	?/neutral face/yellow sticker
Didn't get it/totally lost	#&/frowning face/red sticker

Some teachers simply have students fill in the blanks of a few short statements like these:

The part of the assignment I understood best was

_____ .

I was confused when _____ .
I need help with _____ .

One teacher gets feedback from homework by asking her 1st graders to circle the part of the spelling word that is the trickiest. Then she uses that feedback to explain spelling rules to her students. Seventh grade teacher Cryslynn Billingsley wanted students to self-assess by individual concepts, so she created a set of notes and examples of independent, dependent, and subordinate clauses. For homework, students read the notes and put a check mark by what they understood, a question mark by what they "maybe understood," and circled or highlighted parts that were completely foreign to them (Vatterott, 2014).

To get her students comfortable with rubrics, Billingsley distributed eight writing samples and a rubric. Working in groups, students rated which samples were a 1, 2, 3, or 4 on the rubric and then defended their ratings. This practice prepared the students to use the rubric to assess their own writing. The more students self-assess, the more they develop ownership of their learning. As Billingsley explained, "I know they are getting there when they pinpoint where they need work and they use the language of the standards" (Vatterott, 2014). When teachers hear students say, "I need to know more about subordinating conjunctions" or "Integers are why I can't solve equations," they know students are becoming competent at self-assessment.

First graders at Craig Elementary School in Creve Coeur, Missouri, use the reading checklist in Figure 4.6 to self-assess their nonfiction reading. For each set of "I can" statements, students list evidence that shows they have reached the target or check the column marked "not yet." The checklist is the same rubric that is used as the summative assessment for the same learning targets.

When students learn how to take control of their own assessment, they feel more positive about their learning. As Andrade (2007–2008) observed, "Students commented that self-assessment helped them feel prepared, improved the quality of their work, and gave them a better understanding of what they had achieved" (p. 60). And once students are able to self-assess, they can self-monitor their progress on standards, conduct student-led conferences to demonstrate their learning, and set their own goals for improvement. Even very young students can be empowered by tracking their progress. Ashley Brumbaugh, a kindergarten teacher at Rock Island Academy in Rock Island, Illinois, has her kindergarten students create data folders with

FIGURE 4.6
Navigating Nonfiction Reading Checklist: 1st Grade

I can:	Here is my evidence:	Yes	Not yet
Identify and describe character-istics of nonfiction.			
Ask questions to focus my learning.			
Identify key details.			
Use pictures and words to think about the text.			
Identify a variety of text features.			
Use context clues.			
Use schema.			

Source: © 2014 D. Poslosky, Craig Elementary School, Creve Coeur, Missouri. Used with permission.

graphs showing their progress month by month on the number of sight words, letters, and numbers they know and their mastery of math targets (Vatterott, 2015).

Deemphasizing Grading of Homework

If moving from grading to checking is so positive and empower-ing for students, why would we bother to grade homework at all? Actually, many teachers around the world do not grade home-work. According to a comparison of 50 countries, U.S. teachers lead the world in the grading of homework. Almost 70 percent of U.S. teachers use homework to calculate student grades, com-pared with 28 percent in Canada and 14 percent in Japan (Baker & LeTendre, 2005). As discussed earlier, grading plays a huge role in the old homework paradigm; homework grades are used to reward the virtue of turning work in on time and to punish the vice of perceived laziness—so much so that teachers will say, "If I don't grade it, they won't do it." Yet even with grades, some students fail to complete homework. And in schools in which homework is not graded, students are still expected to complete it, and teachers still struggle to find ways to get the work done. Grading is so much a part of the old paradigm that teachers may become very upset at the idea of *not grading* homework.

The Concept of Grading Homework Dies Hard

In one district, high school teachers who counted homework heavily in the grades they gave protested when the middle school decided *not* to count homework in grades. The high school teachers believed that if the middle school teachers didn't count homework as part of the grade or if they allowed students to redo homework, they would be setting the students up for failure in the high school because homework *did* count in the high school grades. What was particularly interesting was how passionately teachers felt about the necessity of grading homework.

"At the last meeting, one high school teacher about jumped out of her skin. The idea that every homework assignment wouldn't count as part of the final grade was inconceivable," according to another teacher. Members of the district committee worked hard to convince other teachers that grades must be based on how well the students *learned* what they were supposed to. The committee finally agreed that behaviors should not be part of grades and that pre-tests, first attempts, and practice should not be averaged into the grade.

The goal is to have grades reflect learning, not behavior or personal responsibility (Brookhart, 2017). What if grades reflected what students really learned, not which work they chose or were able to complete?

The current consensus is that homework should be formative assessment that helps prepare students for summative assessment. Therefore, in a truly standards-based system, homework is not graded. Homework is reviewed and feedback is given, but not counted in the grade. Completion of homework can be reported separately on the report card as a work habit (more about standards-based homework policies in Chapter 5). Because students typically don't see how homework connects to summative assessments, it needs to be made explicit. To explain the logic of this practice to students as well as parents, the following statements are helpful:

- Does it count? Yes, because it helps you pass the test or complete the paper.
- If it doesn't count, there is no motivation to cheat or for parents to be overly involved; the motivation is to pass the assessment.
- Accountability comes when you pass or fail the assessment (it's delayed gratification). (Vatterott, 2015)

Questions—And More Questions

"If homework doesn't count in the grade, then what would we grade?" This question arose from teachers in a staff development session about homework, which led the presenter to ask this question: "What *are* teachers grading?" It appeared that some teachers at this school graded only tests and homework. Why weren't they grading tasks that students did in class? Perhaps because they were primarily lecturing and having discussions and not providing many learning activities during class time that could be evaluated.

This led to a broader discussion. "What are you doing with grades? What do grades mean to you?" The discussion with this group of teachers revealed a larger problem. They viewed grades as a commodity—they needed a certain number of grades in the gradebook to feel secure. They needed a certain number of grades to please parents. They just needed to make sure they had enough *things* to grade. What they had failed to consider was whether the grades represented learning and how many grades students needed in order to know how they were doing. The teachers had failed to focus on which tasks accurately reflected student learning.

Decriminalizing Late Work

If the purpose of homework is to enhance learning and provide feedback about learning, then the goal is for the homework to be completed—better late than never. But for some teachers, homework is more about their control and convenience than about learning. One teacher explained, "I will not accept late work past two days. Any later and the students end up creating their own time schedule, do what they want when they want, and it's not worth (time-wise) going back and grading something you've moved past." For those teachers who feel compelled to punish the vice of lateness, there is a kinder, gentler way than the old policy that says "50 percent off if it's one day late." Policies like that are an insult to the time and energy the student put forth to complete the assignment. Many a student has simply said, "No way—I am not doing that much work for half credit," and the assignment is never done.

If homework must count in the grade, the general philosophy is this: First, do no harm—don't kill motivation or course grades by being too punitive. To encourage students to do the work, it's better to provide a more generous time limit with fewer points lost than to punish the student for not following the rules. Remember that the goal is learning, not control or compliance. If the teacher needs feedback right away, to know how well the student understood the concept, he or she may require the student to complete an abbreviated version of the homework task in class.

Ideally, homework should not count in the final grade—but in reality, in many schools it still does. This may be a result of the tradition of grading all work (rewarding working instead of learning), mistrust of students to work without grades, or even pressure from parents. If we must put grades for homework in the gradebook to satisfy parents or policy, there is a way to "grade" in a nonthreatening manner. Some teachers give number grades for homework to document completion but treat them as no-counts—temporary grades that carry zero weight in determining the final grade (Vatterott, 2015).

As more and more schools move to standards-based report cards, homework grades may become obsolete. If the goal is mastery of the standard, would it matter if or when homework was completed? Mastery of standards would be based on in-class assessments, with homework used to prepare students to pass the assessment. Homework would be necessary only to master individual standards; if students tested out of some standards, no homework would be necessary for that content.

Summing Up

Most teachers were never trained in effective homework practices. As a result, traditional practices, such as assigning the same homework to all students and giving zeros for incomplete homework, are still common. Many of those traditional practices, however, have not supported learning for all students. The new homework paradigm introduced in this chapter focuses on designing quality homework tasks, differentiating those tasks, deemphasizing grading, improving homework completion, and providing homework support programs.

Homework should not occur in isolation but be closely connected to classroom learning. The purpose of homework is to *support* classroom learning through prelearning, diagnosis, checking for understanding, practice, and processing. When classroom learning and homework are carefully planned, the pieces of the puzzle fit together nicely; homework is used as *formative assessment*—to check for understanding before practice is assigned, to determine how much practice is needed to perfect a skill, and to judge the student's depth of understanding and ability to apply learning.

Viewing homework as formative feedback changes our perspective on the grading of homework. Grading becomes not only unnecessary for feedback, but possibly even detrimental to the student's continued motivation to learn. With this new perspective, incomplete homework is not punished with failing grades but is viewed as a symptom of a learning problem that requires investigation, diagnosis, and support. Strategies for improving homework completion and homework support programs and policies are discussed in Chapter 5.

Homework Completion Strategies and Support Programs

Chapter 4 discussed the first four steps of the new homework paradigm: designing and differentiating quality homework tasks, moving from grading to checking, and deemphasizing grading. These strategies make homework tasks more pleasant and less punitive, and they increase student ownership of homework. These changes from traditional practice should make completion of homework less of an issue. In Chapter 5, we consider the last two steps in the new homework paradigm: using strategies for homework completion and establishing programs that support students in completing homework at school.

Attitudes About Homework Completion

Before we attempt to improve the rate of homework completion, we must confront one more traditional attitude. It is common for teachers to become obsessed with the fact that "all homework must be done." But does it truly need to be done? Some teachers will say, "I gave them a job and they didn't do it." But that is the *old* paradigm. In the new paradigm, it's not about finishing the work; it's about demonstrating learning. Can students prove that they know what they need to know? How can we determine how well they are learning, and how can we help them do better? If we can assess learning without all those homework assignments and the students have learned what we wanted them to learn, we don't need the homework! This is a hard pill to swallow if we believe that students must do as they are told, and that not completing all homework is a sign of laziness or insubordination. But when we become so concerned that children have not been compliant, we lose sight of the role homework should play in learning. Focused on enforcing our own power as teachers, we become afraid to trust students, afraid they're going to get away with something—so we sometimes resort to punitive solutions that backfire. When judging the importance of homework completion, teachers should consider whether they are focusing on compliance without evidence that the tasks are crucial to reaching the learning goal.

Diagnosing Completion Problems

Often when students do not complete homework, the teacher's first reaction is to ask "How do I make them do it?" or to blame the students or their parents for not being compliant. Neither of these gets to the root of the issue; lack of homework completion is symptomatic of other problems. Assuming the homework is meaningful and not busywork, the first step in improving homework completion is to diagnose *why* the homework is not getting done. There are usually five types of reasons:

- *Academic*—Either the task is too hard or too lengthy for the student's working speed, or the task is too easy and has already been mastered.
- *Organizational*—The student is having trouble getting it home, getting it done, or getting it back.

- *Motivational*—The student is experiencing burnout, overload, too much failure, or frustration with tasks.
- *Situational*—The student is unable to work at home, has too many other activities, or lacks materials at home for the assignment.
- *Personal*—The student is experiencing a personal issue such as depression, anxiety, or family problems.

Both academic and motivational issues can be influenced by the quality or type of homework tasks students are assigned. As teachers, we often assume that our homework tasks are foolproof—that it has to be *that task* that the student must complete. Diagnosis is not only about why the student didn't do the homework, but also about the suitability of the task and the degree of ownership students are granted. If there are alternatives to the original task—perhaps shorter or different tasks that will accomplish the same result—then why not allow them? If David, a 6th grader, puts off doing homework because the tasks he is assigned are boring and tedious, the problem is with the task, not the student. If learning has been adequately individualized (as discussed in Chapter 4) with relevant and high-interest tasks, will homework completion even be a problem?

Academic and organizational issues may be easier to diagnose than motivational, situational, or personal issues; it often takes a bit of detective work to determine the problem. Jason, a 3rd grader, has both academic and motivational reasons for not completing homework. He avoids homework because the tasks are so difficult that he feels frustrated and incompetent. Amanda has organizational problems with long-range projects. As a 4th grader, she has had little experience or guidance in budgeting time and setting intermittent deadlines for herself. At her age, time is an abstract concept, and three weeks seems like an infinite amount of time to finish a project. Nathan's problems are situational: as a popular 10th grader, he first makes time for sports and his social life, leaving little time for homework, his last priority.

Each student's situation is unique, and sometimes the student has more than one issue contributing to the problem.

Why Isn't Laura Turning In Homework?

Laura is a bright, sociable 7th grader who just wouldn't keep up with her homework. Earlier in the school year, Laura seemed to be breezing right through the regular homework, so her academic team of teachers decided she should be doing more challenging homework instead. That's when the problems started. Laura seemed to take no initiative to do the work yet appeared to feel guilty when she did not have homework to turn in. She was testing poorly. Her parents claimed she locked herself in her room for four hours a night doing homework, but they seemed powerless to monitor whether she was actually working during that time. They promised to get more involved but did not. They continued to make excuses for why Laura was not completing homework (situational).

Upon further investigation, the team discovered Laura was struggling with the challenge homework (academic), was feeling overwhelmed (motivational), and was free to chat with friends on social media while locked in her room (situational). Due to her lack of organization, she often completed work that never made it back to the teacher (organizational).

The teachers decided to take the parents out of the equation and deal directly with Laura. They followed three simple steps. First, they went back to giving her regular homework assignments instead of challenge work, at least until they reestablished the pattern of her getting all the work back and saw her test grades improve. Second, upon talking with Laura, they discovered that she didn't like to put work in folders as suggested by her teachers, and work often got lost as a result. When asked what might work better, she said she preferred to fold the work and put it in her textbook. This simple change helped Laura become more organized because it gave her the control she needed to do what made sense to her. Finally, because Laura was not self-motivated to complete work, the teachers assigned her to a mandatory after-school homework support program until she developed a track record of turning in all work. After that they periodically placed Laura back in the homework support program as needed, before she was missing too many assignments.

Diagnostic Tools

In many cases, a simple conversation with the student may give us the insight we need to diagnose the cause of problems with homework completion. The tools described here can also be helpful.

- *Parent or student feedback checklists* can help us determine how much time students are spending on homework and the reasons why work is not being completed. Using the checklists daily for a short period should reveal what difficulties the student is having. Depending on the age and maturity of the student and the level of involvement of the parent, the checklist may be directed to either the student or the parent. (See Figure 5.1 for a student feedback checklist; a parent feedback checklist is shown in Figure 2.4 in Chapter 2.)
- A *home study plan* (see Figure 5.2) helps students reflect on the conditions under which they work best. It helps students and parents determine the best time and place for homework to be completed.
- *Taylor's Homework Chain* (Figure 5.3) was created for students with attention deficit disorder, but it can be helpful for any student with organizational problems. It helps students to self-diagnose where organization is breaking down in the process of getting homework completed and turned in (Taylor, 2007).

Prioritizing Concepts, Tasks, and Subjects

If, after diagnosis and adjustment of homework for a student's specific needs, the student is still consistently not completing all work, it may be that the student is a slow worker. In that case, it may be necessary to prioritize concepts within a subject. Prioritizing can be done by identifying mastery and nonmastery concepts and, when the student begins to get behind, excusing some of the nonmastery concepts. Some teachers feel this is letting

FIGURE 5.1
Student Feedback Checklist

Dear student:

I estimate you can complete this assignment in _____ minutes.
It is not necessary for you to work longer than _____ minutes on this assignment, even if you do not finish it. You will not be penalized.

How much time did you spend on this assignment?_____
If you did not finish the assignment, please check the reason or reasons why below:

_____ I could no longer focus on the task.

_____ I was too tired.

_____ I did not understand the assignment.

_____ I did not have the necessary materials to complete the assignment.

_____ I did not have enough time due to other outside activities.

_____ Other reason (please explain)._____

Student signature_____

FIGURE 5.2
Home Study Plan

We all have ways we like to work. These questions will help you figure out the best way to do homework. Circle the answer that is most like you. (For prereaders, read questions and have students draw their answers.)

1. My favorite position to do homework is . . .

    At a desk.
    Sitting on the floor.
    Standing.
    Lying down.

2. It is easiest for me to pay attention to homework . . .

    In a quiet place.
    With noise or music in the background.

3. When I am working on homework . . .

    I need to have something to eat or drink.
    I don't need to have drinks or food.

4. When I have more than one thing to do . . .

    I like to do the easiest thing first.
    I like to do the hardest thing first.

5. After I start working, I like to . . .

    Work for a long time before I take a break.
    Work for a short time, take a break, then work more.

continued

FIGURE 5.2 (*continued*)
Home Study Plan

6. When is it easiest for me to do homework?

   I like to work as soon as I get home from school.
   I need to play or relax for a little while and then work.
   I need a long break after school before I am ready to work.

7. Where will I do homework?

   I can work in the same place every day and can keep my homework things
   there. That place is _____

   _____.

   I have to work in different places on different days, so I need to keep my
   homework things in a box that I can move. Some of the places I will work
   are_____

   _____

   _____

   _____.

FIGURE 5.3
Taylor's Homework Chain

Which links are weak or broken?

[ ] 1. Realize an assignment is being given.

[ ] 2. Understand the assignment.

[ ] 3. Record the assignment accurately.

[ ] 4. Understand how to perform the assignment correctly.

[ ] 5. Check to bring correct books home.

[ ] 6. Arrive home with materials and the homework assignment.

[ ] 7. Begin the homework session.

[ ] 8. Complete all homework.

[ ] 9. Check that it is complete, accurate, and neat.

[ ] 10. Set completed homework in a special place.

[ ] 11. Take completed homework to school.

[ ] 12. Arrive at class with completed homework.

[ ] 13. Turn completed homework in on time.

Source: From *Motivating the Uncooperative Student: Redeeming Discouragement and Attitude Problems,* by J. Taylor, 2007, Monmouth, OR: ADD Plus. Copyright © 2007 by ADD Plus. Adapted with permission.

students off too easy, but if the students are slower learners, they simply may not have enough time. A useful analogy might be this: Suppose a student missed a month of school because he was sick. Wouldn't we just excuse some work and evaluate him only on what he had done?

One teacher made this comment: "If you prioritize tasks, you'll probably realize the task at the bottom of the list isn't worth doing and should be dropped." For students with multiple learning deficits, prioritizing homework in different subjects is essential to avoid overburdening the students. For each of those students, teachers must answer the following question: "What are the most critical subjects for future success?" For instance, if reading comprehension is a problem, it affects all content learning and must take priority. If basic math skills are hampering the student's ability to perform higher operations, those basic skills must be priorities. The dilemma comes in the prioritizing of individual academic subjects. Should math and reading be prioritized over science and social studies? Should homework in the four academic subjects be prioritized over homework in the elective subjects? The balancing of priorities is a difficult job that may require the collaboration of several teachers.

General Classroom Strategies for Homework Completion

All students benefit from a consistent routine such as having homework on the same days of the week, or always having math homework on Mondays and reading homework on Tuesdays. Younger students benefit from homework in the same format, such as five practice problems followed by five review problems.

Many students in elementary and middle school need help in organization. It is usually worth the time to teach students specific organizational strategies and to schedule a regular time for them to organize folders or clean out lockers. Middle school teachers who schedule weekly locker clean-outs find many homework assignments in the process! Some high school students still require this type of monitoring and organizational help.

A visual chart of completed homework is a concrete way for students to track their work. Having students keep an individual record or graph of how many assignments they have turned in on time is one approach. One teacher keeps a record of her 9th graders' homework completion on a wall poster. Students are identified with a PIN they select. They can then check the chart at any time to see what assignments they may be missing. One 2nd grade teacher had students make a bar graph showing the number of students who turned in their homework each day. The simple visual of the bars seemed to increase the number of students who turned in work. The names of the students who did not turn in work were not revealed or placed on the graph, as that would have been punitive and embarrassing for those students.

For many students, posting assignments online or on their devices ensures they know what their homework assignment is. For students without access to technology, hard copies of home-work assignments should be available. If that is not an option, the teacher may write the assignment on the board and check to make sure all students have copied the assignment. Some students may need to receive a written copy or have a buddy write down the assignment for them. Wise teachers avoid giving homework assignments verbally—it takes only a few seconds of distraction for students to miss it entirely!

Other strategies that may improve the rate of homework completion are the following:

- Limit homework to one assignment or one subject per night.
- When the purpose of the homework is to check for under-standing of today's lesson, consider assigning it at the beginning of the class.

- Take time to discuss the homework assignment and possibly give students a few minutes to begin the assignment in class. This way, students can be sure they understand what they are supposed to do.
- Avoid giving homework assignments at the end of the hour, when students are packing up and focused on leaving.
- Set a maximum amount of time that students should work on each assignment.
- Provide peer tutors or study groups for some students.
- Assign students homework buddies to work with or call for help.
- Give assignments further in advance of the due date, or give students more than one day to do assignments.
- Provide homework packets or lists of weekly assignments.
- Give all assignments for the next week on Friday, due the next Friday.
- Establish intermittent due dates for parts of long-term projects.
- Allow some homework to lag two to three weeks behind the introduction of a concept to check for understanding (like a take-home test).
- Make sure all students have the necessary materials at home to complete specific assignments.

Here are some home-based strategies to improve completion of homework:

- Use the parent or student feedback checklists (Figures 2.4 and 5.1, respectively) for students who repeatedly have completion problems.
- Use the home study plan (Figure 5.2) to help students create the best homework environment at home.
- Use Taylor's Homework Chain (Figure 5.3) to diagnose students with organizational problems.

- Use the home schedule card for parents (Figure 2.2) to determine if some students need more flexibility in homework deadlines.
- Give some students a copy of the textbook to keep at home.
- Allow parents or students to call the teacher at home when necessary.
- Have younger students make and decorate a "homework box" to keep materials in at home.
- Give parents specific guidelines on *how* to help with homework and *how much* to help (see example in Figure 2.1).

Establishing Homework Support Programs

Teachers who use some of the completion strategies just described and who stay after school or give up their lunch period to help students complete homework provide their own form of homework support. School-sanctioned homework support programs extend that help in a broader, more organized fashion. Homework support programs allow us to save students from themselves and make it difficult for them to fail. These programs allow us to "bird-dog" students to make sure they complete the work necessary to succeed. If they are inefficient or unmotivated learners, doesn't it make sense that they would need to do homework at school in a structured support program, where they could get expert one-on-one help? If students need extra help with homework, it is the obligation of the school to provide that help, not outside tutoring services.

But homework support programs are no magic bullet and certainly no remedy for busywork. Support programs focus on completion, but in isolation. They fail to take into account *why* students are not completing homework—the diagnosis is missing. Ideally, homework support programs should be used in conjunction with the previously discussed teacher strategies for differentiation, diagnosis, and completion. Also, homework support programs work only if students are given a reasonable amount of *meaningful* homework. If students are assigned several hours of nightly homework, a homework support program alone will not save them.

The most successful programs kick in when a student is missing only 2 or 3 assignments, not 9 or 10. Once students become backlogged with too many missing assignments, the job of catching up becomes laborious and the prospect of reaching the goal bleak.

The Philosophy Behind Successful Support Programs

A successful homework support program is not just about homework. It is a reflection of a school philosophy of high expectations for all, a respect for students' innate desire to succeed, and a comprehensive approach that actively monitors student performance and mandates additional help when needed (Perkins-Gough, 2006). It represents a no-excuses, whatever-it-takes attitude on the part of the faculty and administrators.

Homework support programs are more effective when the attitudes and intentions of teachers and administrators are about helping rather than punishing. Attitudes and intentions are revealed to students in formal policy statements about the support programs, in the way teachers communicate to students referred to the program, and in how students are treated when working in the program. The heart of a successful support program is just that—heart. It is a deep compassion for students that reveals itself in a helping, not punishing, attitude. After-school support programs often provide water and snacks for students, and some after-school programs include recreational activities in addition to homework help.

When and Why Homework Support Programs Are Needed

When designing a homework support program for a school or district, we come to a philosophical fork in the road. A fundamental question drives such a program's design and implementation: what is the goal of the program—completion or mastery?

Traditional homework support programs were simplistic, focused solely on making up the missing work with no regard for the stage learners were at, their working speed, the way they learned best, or whether they really needed to do the work. If the goal of the homework support program is to provide time and space for students to complete all assigned work, yet some students are perpetually behind, then those students need further diagnosis and differentiation to meet their learning needs. Here's one idea to formalize that diagnosis: after a student has been referred to a support program five times for incomplete homework, teachers are asked to make an action plan specifically for that student. That plan might include such interventions as

- Testing for skill level, academic gaps, or learner strengths.
- Testing for learning disabilities.
- Reducing the length of homework tasks.
- Creating alternative task choices.
- Conferencing with the student or his or her parents.
- "Forgiving" some backlogged work (e.g., complete two missing assignments, forgive five), especially when incomplete homework is a result of frequent absences.
- Revising classroom management strategies if missing work is primarily a result of the student not working during class.

If a school or teacher has implemented standards-based learning, completion of all homework may not matter. What matters is whether the student can demonstrate the understanding or skill that each standard addresses. In a standards-based system, homework support is targeted—specific to the learning standards the student has not yet mastered. The goal is to provide additional time for learning or remediation for retesting. A support program provides the time and place to complete necessary tasks to qualify for retesting. Whether the program is *homework support* (to complete all the work), *learning support* (to master specific standards), or a combination of both, support programs are about time—structured, supervised time during or after school. The structures discussed here could be used for either purpose.

Schoolwide homework support programs generally fall into one of three categories: options that find time during the school day, curricular and scheduling options, and after-school support programs. The trend has been to move away from punitive programs that focus only on homework completion and toward programs that focus more broadly on academic success, with homework as just one component.

Options That Find Time During the School Day

Lunch and homework. Assigning students to complete homework during lunch is one of the most common forms of homework support. It can be used as soon as work is late, and work can be made up in a timely manner. Lunchtime seems like a logical time to make up work, although sometimes the teacher loses lunchtime too! The downside to a lunch support program is that, no matter how it's presented, it feels punitive to students. They miss interacting with their friends and don't feel like they've had a break. (How much less efficient are *we* later in the day when we work through lunch?) An occasional session could be helpful for students, but if a student is repeatedly working during the lunch break, it's not working and it's interfering with the student's needs for downtime and socializing. With 25-minute lunch periods, the amount of work that is actually accomplished may be minimal, and the sting of missing lunch with friends may create more resentment than it's worth.

Recess and homework. Equally problematic is forcing elementary students to miss recess to make up homework. Again, it seems like a logical place to find some time, albeit only a little. As with lunch programs, missing recess sometimes punishes the teacher as well, and it can hurt student learning later in the day when the student has missed the chance to get some exercise and socialize. Many elementary teachers now refuse to keep students in from recess to make up homework. Many principals have also prohibited the "benching" of students during recess. As one teacher explained, "Ninety-nine percent of the time, those kids who are missing their homework are the kids who most need a break in their day. So by punishing the child, I'm punishing the learning atmosphere in my classroom. It affects my classroom management because this child needed that 15-minute break, and I just took it away from him." Again, this strategy may be effective occasionally, but when overused, both students and parents perceive it to be punitive.

Elementary classroom homework time. The easiest solution in a self-contained elementary classroom is to block out a certain amount of time daily or weekly for students to do homework in class. Faster workers may have some free time, which they could then spend in silent reading, art, peer tutoring, or helping the teacher with classroom responsibilities. Elementary teachers often assign "catch-up time" once a week for the students who need it, while other students have a choice of quiet activities.

Advisory or homeroom time. If the school has a scheduled block of nonacademic time such as an advisory or homeroom period, it can be used for students to receive teacher or peer assistance for homework. If most students are not working on schoolwork during this time, it may be better to have a few teachers assigned specifically to handle homework help. That way, students could be assigned to report to that teacher's classroom for homework help instead of to their homeroom. One teacher per grade level or subject area could serve as the homework help teacher for a month, and the duty could be rotated. Or certain teachers could volunteer to be the homework help teacher for the year and not be assigned an advisory or a homeroom group. Peer tutors could also be used to assist the teachers.

Curricular and Scheduling Options

Monthly late-start day. High school teachers are especially aware of how late teenagers like to stay up at night and how late they like to sleep in the morning. Some schools have instituted once-a-month late-start days, when school starts up to two hours later than normal. The intent is for students to use the extra time to complete overdue homework or work on long-term projects (Pope, 2005).

Weekly homework time. Some schools shorten each class period by a few minutes one day a week to create an hour-long block of time at the end of the school day for homework catch-up. Students stay in their last-period class or report to homeroom for the purpose of completing homework. This weekly opportunity helps to keep students from getting too far behind.

Academic Lab periods. One of the most useful ideas has been the mandatory Academic Lab period. Often used as part of an eight-block high school schedule, students must sign up for one block of Academic Lab each semester. For either 90 minutes every other day or one class period daily, Academic Lab allows students to go to other teachers for help on homework assignments or to get that help from their Academic Lab teacher.

Study hall or independent study courses. Study hall is back! Instead of 100 kids in the cafeteria, though, it's small, focused groups with the ability to travel for help. Study halls are typically offered as noncredit electives, giving students a structured, quiet environment with access to a teacher. At Maplewood Richmond Heights High School in Maplewood, Missouri, most students take a study hall, which has allowed the administration and teachers to "target" the study halls as students need specialized help. Principal Kevin Grawer explained: "I talked to a student who was doing poorly in AP Calculus. I said, 'You're struggling. Let's move you from the physics teacher's study hall to the AP Math teacher's study hall.'" Teachers actively monitor student performance and work with the administration to give students the support they most need.

Alternative strategies or study skills courses. Students who consistently struggle with homework may need instruction in study skills, much like what private tutoring companies offer. These are typically semester-long elective courses, and they may be taught through the communication arts department or by a special education teacher or a teacher of gifted students. In middle schools that offer 6- to 10-week exploratory courses, a 6- to 10-week study skills course may be mandated in place of another exploratory class.

Credit recovery programs. Many high schools offer credit recovery programs, but at Maplewood Richmond Heights High School, credit recovery is competency-based, so students need to make up only the parts of the course they did not master. Students have the choice of working with a teacher or completing an online course.

One-hour lunch period. Some schools have decided that the best way to provide homework help is to add a block of time adjacent to the student lunch period. Students have time to eat, see their friends, and still report to homework help sessions if needed. At Solon High School in Solon, Iowa, a 30-minute intervention period is scheduled immediately before lunch on Tuesdays through Fridays. Even though homework does not count in the grade, students are still expected to complete all of it. But because the school allows remediation and retesting, teachers refer students to intervention both for "skill" (students who need reteaching) and "will" (students who have failed to complete the work).

Extended school day. A solution that seems to be growing in popularity, especially in high-poverty schools, is to extend the school day by 45 minutes or one class period. The extra time is used to coach students academically and to supervise homework. Typically, no additional homework is expected to be completed at home, with the possible exception of reading. An advantage of this plan compared with after-school support programs is that additional transportation is not required.

Before- and After-School Homework Support Programs

After-school support programs are rapidly becoming a popular option for schools struggling with homework issues. As with other support options, they are effective only when students have been given a reasonable amount of meaningful homework and when they are implemented as soon as students are missing only a few assignments. Additional requirements for success are that students are available to stay after school, that parents allow them to stay after school, and that transportation home is provided.

Transportation is a critical component for a viable after-school support program. Logistics are simplified if transportation is already available for other after-school activities. If not, transportation becomes a huge budgetary issue. Many schools use funds from state or federal grants to subsidize transportation. If transportation is not available, some parents will volunteer to pick up their children, but often the child most in need of homework assistance does not have a parent available at that time of day.

Successful after-school support programs can be mandatory, voluntary, or both—mandatory for students who are missing assignments, and voluntary for students who find they work better at school than at home. According to one program director, "Some students voluntarily stay for the mandatory program because they like the quiet atmosphere in which to complete their homework after school."

ZAP (Zeros Aren't Possible or Zeros Aren't Productive) has caught on as a popular name for mandatory after-school homework support programs. Many schools have ZAP programs, but each program may be different. Most operate similarly to the process of assigning detentions, which unfortunately gives the program a punitive feel. When students fail to turn in a home-work assignment, they receive a ZAP form from the teacher and are expected to report to the after-school program.

Highland Middle School in Libertyville, Illinois, calls its homework support program NEST (Needs Extra Study Time). It is offered at lunch and after school to students referred by teachers. In addition, each Friday morning for 30 minutes before school, students can see a teacher without an appointment, as a sort of "office hours" approach to help.

Beyond the Bell is both mandatory and voluntary at Maplewood Richmond Heights High School; students may choose to come on their own or be referred by teachers. The before-school program is for math help only, whereas the after-school program, offered Mondays through Thursdays, rotates math, ELL, and special education teachers.

Marist School, a college preparatory secondary school in Atlanta, Georgia, has tutorial time every day from 3:00 to 3:30. Teachers are in their classrooms available to help students with homework or reteach as necessary. From 3:30 to 4:30 each day, targeted academic support for English/composition, lower- and upper-level mathematics, and science is offered in the Academic Center.

At East Union Elementary School in Afton, Iowa, "after school" homework support takes place every Wednesday from 1:45 to 3:45. The school has early dismissal every Wednesday for teachers' professional development. During this time, the school hires a para-educator to supervise students who have trouble completing required work. That person is also the elementary librarian/para-educator, so she knows all the students well and has knowledge of their reading ability, an added bonus. This is a voluntary program, but parents are typically willing to let their children participate.

Examples of Comprehensive Support Programs

The following examples illustrate how schools can effectively implement and sustain comprehensive homework support programs. These programs actually go beyond homework support to provide broader interventions that help students succeed academically.

Falcon Support was created by the staff of Prairie High School in Battle Ground, Washington, as a support system to improve student learning. It occurs Tuesday and Thursday mornings between 2nd and 3rd period. According to principal Travis Drake, "We seem to have found a nice balance of providing the grade-motivated students an opportunity (and flexibility) to get the help when and where they need it, yet at the same time providing intentional support to the at-risk students."

Here's how it works: Every three weeks, student grades are pulled and the students are divided into two different groups. Students passing all classes or failing only one class are put in the "crimson" group; students failing two or more classes are classified as "gold" (crimson and gold are the school colors).

All "gold" students are assigned an advocate and encouraged to seek out the help they need. Advocates are assigned every six weeks. Students are kept with the same advocate if they continue to stay on the advocate list. The staff has "nesting" meetings every three weeks to assess which interventions are working and to identify any adjustments that need to be made.

During Falcon Support time, "crimson" students have the opportunity to move about the campus and see the teachers they need to see. They also have the freedom to attend club meetings, go to the library or the Career Center, or just hang out in the commons.

Joseph J. Catena Elementary School in Freehold, New Jersey, offers students three opportunities for additional supervised time for homework or remediation (a system made possible by some creative staffing):

- Each day, the students have a 25-minute intervention period during which teachers may reteach some students or provide extension activities for their "high flyers." Students with specific remediation needs can be assigned during that time to the related arts teachers, who work with students on tasks prescribed by the regular classroom teacher (e.g., sight words).
- The Academy is a 45-minute period before school, two days a week. This program, which offers general support, is staffed by the student teachers assigned to the school, who operate the program for 10 of the 15 weeks they are in the school each semester.
- For the third opportunity, the school's Parent-Teacher Organization funds stipends for teachers to staff an after-school Homework Club on Tuesdays and Thursdays. High school students assist the teachers as tutors for community service credit.

Summing Up

The new homework paradigm outlined in this book offers a comprehensive plan for homework reform. But comprehensive reform requires a long-term commitment from teachers, administrators, and parents, and a climate that is open to change. Depending on the unique needs of individual communities, that change may happen quickly or may need to move more slowly. For schools that need time to soften ingrained attitudes, minor changes can be helpful in beginning the process. For those schools, the following "baby steps" may be a good place to start:

- Limit the percentage that homework may count in the grade.
- Revise late policies.
- Limit the number of subjects in which homework is assigned each night.
- Set weekly or nightly time limits.
- Prohibit weekend or holiday homework.

- Coordinate homework with a calendar limiting the number of tests or projects at a given time.
- Limit the number of AP classes that students may take in one semester.

Homework reform is a worthwhile endeavor that has the potential to enhance student learning, reduce failure, improve student motivation, and strengthen the parent-teacher relationship. The key to success is raising awareness, letting go of some traditional attitudes and practices, and putting the well-being of children first.

Afterword

Homework is a unique educational practice. Of all the learning strategies a teacher may use, it is the only one encompassing the two worlds of school and home that all children inhabit. Given the complexity of family life and the diversity of students today, it is no surprise that the practice of homework is challenging—and in some communities, controversial.

The scope of our challenges reflects the wide social and economic diversity of our schools. Our challenges range from reeling in the extreme homework overload (wrongly equated with rigor) that is often prevalent in highly competitive schools, to helping teachers in impoverished schools who struggle to get students to complete even the simplest of homework tasks. Our frustrations are compounded by the nagging feeling that, if we could just get it right, homework could be a real asset to learning. Our instincts are not wrong.

At its best, homework in reasonable amounts can support and enhance learning, provide feedback to teachers about learning, allow students to practice skills and deepen their knowledge, and instill confidence within students when they successfully complete tasks on their own.

But at its worst, homework may widen the achievement gap and unfairly discriminate against students who are unable to work at home. At its worst, homework may dampen student enthusiasm and love of learning and may lead to frustration and feelings of incompetence. When homework is excessive, it may compromise the healthy balance among work, play, and down-time that all children need.

To improve homework practices, we must

- First acknowledge our inborn attitudes about homework and question the folklore behind homework traditions.
- Examine homework research with a critical eye and trust what our experience with learners has taught us.
- Accept not only that parenting and families have changed, but also that the relationship between parents and schools has changed. We must respect the right of parents to control their child's free time, and we must work cooperatively with parents to determine homework guidelines.

To implement homework effectively, we must

- Connect homework to classroom learning and clearly identify the purpose of each assignment.
- Provide students with relevant tasks that they can complete without adult help.
- Use what we know about learning to design homework appropriate for individual students.
- Facilitate two-way communication between teachers and students and between teachers and parents.
- Respect the role of motivation and winning streaks in the decisions that students make to tackle and persist with homework tasks.

To implement homework equitably, we must

- Assign reasonable amounts of homework.
- Differentiate homework for individual needs.
- Be sensitive about the limitations of home environments.
- Accept that not all students can or will work at home.
- Remove failure as an option by minimizing or eliminating the grading of homework.

• Establish school-sponsored homework support programs.

Homework reform can be a wonderful catalyst for total school reform. An examination of homework practices may jump-start conversations about curriculum standards, grading practices, and teaching strategies. Reform of homework practices may drive future reform of assessment, curriculum, and instructional practices.

But the journey of homework reform is not a simple one. Along the way there will be resistance, roadblocks to change, and a wide diversity of opinions. Parents, teachers, or administrators may cling to outdated beliefs, or they may be mired in the inertia of old habits. Consensus may be difficult as we struggle to find that common ground where school and family values intersect. But within the context of the needs of individual communities and the reality of family's everyday lives, consensus can be found.

You are not alone in your quest for change—thousands of schools around the world have changed their homework practices, and many more have begun the process of reform. So stay the course and keep the faith. You are undoing 100 years of traditional attitudes and beliefs to provide more meaningful learning experiences for your students. It is valuable and important work.

Homework Survey for Students (Short Version)

Difficulty of homework

(Circle "agree" or "disagree" or write a comment.)

1. When I have homework in **math** . . .
    - I understand the reason for doing the assignment.

    agree   disagree   comment _____

    - Most of the time the homework is easy.

    agree   disagree   comment _____

    - Sometimes assignments are so hard, I get frustrated.

    agree   disagree   comment _____

    - I am often confused about what I am supposed to do.

    agree   disagree   comment _____

2. When I have homework in **science** . . .
    - I understand the reason for doing the assignment.

    agree   disagree   comment _____

    - Most of the time the homework is easy.

    agree   disagree   comment _____

    - Sometimes assignments are so hard, I get frustrated.

    agree   disagree   comment _____

• I am often confused about what I am supposed to do.

agree   disagree   comment _____

3. When I have homework in **social studies** . . .
  • I understand the reason for doing the assignment.

agree   disagree   comment _____

  • Most of the time the homework is easy.

agree   disagree   comment _____

  • Sometimes assignments are so hard, I get frustrated.

agree   disagree   comment _____

  • I am often confused about what I am supposed to do.

agree   disagree   comment _____

4. When I have homework in **language arts/reading** . . .
  • I understand the reason for doing the assignment.

agree   disagree   comment _____

  • Most of the time the homework is easy.

agree   disagree   comment _____

  • Sometimes assignments are so hard, I get frustrated.

agree   disagree   comment _____

  • I am often confused about what I am supposed to do.

agree   disagree   comment _____

Staying organized

5. How often do these things happen to you? (Circle one answer for each statement.)
  • I find out we had homework last night, but I didn't know about it.

all the time   most of the time   sometimes   never

- I don't have enough time to write down the homework assignment.

all the time　　most of the time　　sometimes　　never

- I forget to write down the homework assignment.

all the time　　most of the time　　sometimes　　never

- I forget something I need to do my homework (like books or my notebook).

all the time　　most of the time　　sometimes　　never

- I don't have time at the end of the day to get everything I need for homework.

all the time　　most of the time　　sometimes　　never

- I do the homework but forget to turn it in.

all the time　　most of the time　　sometimes　　never

- I know I did a homework assignment, but I can't find it.

all the time　　most of the time　　sometimes　　never

Getting it done

6. Which statement sounds most like you? (Check one.)

___ I usually get all my homework done.

___ I usually *don't* get all my homework done.

___ Sometimes I get all my homework done, sometimes I don't.

7. When I have trouble getting my homework done, it's because . . . (Check all that apply to you.)

___ I don't have a quiet place to work.

___ There are too many distractions at home.

___ I can't concentrate.

___ I'm tired.

___ I don't know what I'm supposed to do.

___ My homework is too hard.

___ I need help, but my parents don't have time to help me.

___ I need help, but my parents don't understand the assignment.

___ My school medicine has worn off.

___ I just run out of time.

___ I have things I need to do around the house (like chores, cooking, or babysitting).

___ I have activities I need to go to (like sports, music, or religion lessons).

___ Other reasons (please explain):_____

APPENDIX B
Homework Survey for Students

The purpose of this survey is to learn more about homework practices in your school and to find out your opinions about homework. Parents and teachers will also be asked to complete surveys. All surveys are anonymous. Do not put your name on this survey.

Basic information

What grade are you in?_____

What is your sex?_____

Do you receive special education help?
(Circle one.)   Yes   No   I don't know

Are you in the gifted program?
(Circle one.)   Yes   No   I don't know

Time spent on homework

1. About how much time do you spend on homework each night?

2. What do you think is a fair amount of homework for you each night? Why?

3. How often do you have homework in **math**? (Check one answer.)

___ Every night

___ Two or three nights a week

___ Once a week

___ Less than once a week

4. How often do you have homework in **science**? (Check one answer.)

___ Every night

___ Two or three nights a week

___ Once a week

___ Less than once a week

5. How often do you have homework in **social studies**? (Check one answer.)

___ Every night

___ Two or three nights a week

___ Once a week

___ Less than once a week

6. How often do you have homework in **language arts or reading**? (Check one answer.)

___ Every night

___ Two or three nights a week

___ Once a week

___ Less than once a week

7. Estimate how many minutes you usually spend **each night on each subject**.

____ minutes on math

____ minutes on science

____ minutes on social studies

____ minutes on language arts/reading

Purpose of homework

8. What do you think is the reason for most homework?

Difficulty of homework

These questions are about how easy or hard different types of homework are for you. You will answer the same set of questions for each subject. Please answer these questions by circling "agree" or "disagree" or by writing a comment.

9. When I have homework in **math** . . .

  • I understand the reason for doing the assignment.

agree   disagree   comment_____

  • Most of the time the homework is easy.

agree   disagree   comment_____

  • Sometimes assignments are so hard, I get frustrated.

agree   disagree   comment_____

  • I am often confused about what I am supposed to do.

agree   disagree   comment_____

10. When I have homework in **science** . . .

  • I understand the reason for doing the assignment.

agree   disagree   comment_____

- Most of the time the homework is easy.

agree   disagree   comment _____

- Sometimes assignments are so hard, I get frustrated.

agree   disagree   comment _____

- I am often confused about what I am supposed to do.

agree   disagree   comment _____

11. When I have homework in **social studies** . . .
   - I understand the reason for doing the assignment.

agree   disagree   comment _____

   - Most of the time the homework is easy.

agree   disagree   comment _____

   - Sometimes assignments are so hard, I get frustrated.

agree   disagree   comment _____

   - I am often confused about what I am supposed to do.

agree   disagree   comment _____

12. When I have homework in **language arts/reading** . . .
   - I understand the reason for doing the assignment.

agree   disagree   comment _____

   - Most of the time the homework is easy.

agree   disagree   comment _____

   - Sometimes assignments are so hard, I get frustrated.

agree   disagree   comment _____

   - I am often confused about what I am supposed to do.

agree   disagree   comment _____

Staying organized

13. How often do these things happen to you? (Circle one answer for each statement.)

• I find out we had homework last night, but I didn't know about it.

all the time   most of the time   sometimes   never

• I don't have enough time to write down the homework assignment.

all the time   most of the time   sometimes   never

• I forget to write down the homework assignment.

all the time   most of the time   sometimes   never

• I forget something I need to do my homework (like books or my notebook).

all the time   most of the time   sometimes   never

• I don't have time at the end of the day to get everything I need for homework.

all the time   most of the time   sometimes   never

• I do the homework but forget to turn it in.

all the time   most of the time   sometimes   never

• I know I did a homework assignment, but I can't find it.

all the time   most of the time   sometimes   never

Getting it done

14. Which statement sounds most like you? (Check one.)

___ I usually get all my homework done.

___ I usually *don't* get all my homework done.

___ Sometimes I get all my homework done, sometimes I don't.

15. When I have trouble getting my homework done, it's because
. . . (Check all that apply to you.)

___ I don't have a quiet place to work.

___ There are too many distractions at home.

___ I can't concentrate.

___ I'm tired.

___ I don't know what I'm supposed to do.

___ My homework is too hard.

___ I need help, but my parents don't have time to help me.

___ I need help, but my parents don't understand the assignment.

___ My school medicine has worn off.

___ I just run out of time.

___ I have things I need to do around the house (like chores, cooking, or babysitting).

___ I have activities I need to go to (like sports, music, or religion lessons).

___ Other reasons (please explain):_____

Other questions about homework

16. How do you think homework helps your learning?

17. Are there times when you think homework hurts your learning? If so, how?

18. Does homework affect how you feel about the subject? How?

19. Does homework affect how you feel about the teacher? How?

20. Does homework cause problems in your family? If so, please explain.

21. What could your teachers do to make homework better and less stressful?

22. Is there anything else you would like your teacher to know about homework?

Homework Survey for Teachers

The purpose of this survey is to learn more about homework practices in your school and to find out your opinions about homework. Students and parents will also be asked to complete surveys. All surveys are anonymous.

Grade level(s) taught_____

Subject(s) taught_____

Number of years of teaching experience_____

1. How many nights a week do you assign homework (Monday through Thursday)?

2. Do you assign homework on weekends or over school vacations?

3. Why do you assign homework? (Check all that apply.)

___ For practice of a skill

___ To check for understanding

___ To prepare students for the next day's lesson

___ To teach students responsibility

___ Other instructional reasons (please list) _____

_____

___ Because I feel pressure from other teachers

___ Because I feel pressure from the administration

___ Because it is school policy

___ Because I feel pressure from parents

___ Other noninstructional reasons (please list)_____

4. How well does homework work? How effective is homework in reaching the goals listed above?

5. In your opinion, is homework an important part of the learning process? Why?

6. What percentage of your students turn in homework assignments on time?

7. What percentage of your students turn in homework assignments late?

8. What percentage of your students rarely or never turn in homework?

9. For those students who consistently fail to turn in homework, to what do you attribute the problem?

10. What strategies do you find effective in getting students to do their homework?

11. Do you think homework creates resentment in parents?

12. How do your students receive feedback about homework?

13. Do you grade homework? If so, how? (e.g., number grades, letter grades, for completeness only)

14. If you grade homework, what percentage is it of the student's quarter grade?

15. In a typical quarter, approximately how many of your students earn *D*s or *F*s for their quarter grade?

16. Of those *D* and *F* students, what percentage of them fail primarily due to incomplete homework?

Homework Survey for Parents

The purpose of this survey is to learn more about homework practices in your school and to find out your opinions about homework. Teachers and students will also be asked to complete surveys. All surveys are anonymous.

Basic information

Grade level of child_____

Sex of child_____

Does your child receive special education services? (Circle one.)   Yes   No   I don't know

Does your child participate in the gifted program? (Circle one.)   Yes   No   I don't know

Time spent on homework

1. On average, how much time does your child spend on homework on weekday evenings?

2. On average, how much time does your child spend on homework on weekends?

3. What do you feel is an appropriate amount of homework for your child's grade level?

4. How do you feel about weekend homework and homework over holiday vacations?

5. How much control should parents have over the amount of homework their child has? (Check all that apply to your child.)

___ I should be able to request a limit on the amount of homework.

___ I should be able to request a limit on the time spent on homework.

___ I should be able to request modifications in the difficulty of assignments.

___ I should be able to request additional homework for my child.

___ I should be able to excuse my child from homework when I feel it is necessary.

___ The amount and type of homework is up to the teacher.

Other _____

Purpose or value of homework

6. How often do you understand the value of the homework assignment to your child's learning?

7. How often does the homework appear to be busywork?

Difficulty of homework/child's work habits

8. Can your child complete homework without your help or supervision?

___ Yes, always

___ Yes, usually

___ Yes, but doesn't want to

___ Not usually

___ Never

Other _____

9. Does your child have special needs or special circumstances that influence his or her ability to complete homework? (Check all that apply to your child.)

___ My child takes medication for school that has worn off before homework is done.

___ My child needs a lot of downtime to relax after a hard day at school.

___ My child has many responsibilities at home that leave little time for homework.

___ My child is involved in many outside activities that leave little time for homework.

___ My child spends little time at home on weekdays because of extended day care, babysitters, or visitation with noncustodial parents.

Other _____

10. If your child has difficulty working alone, to what do you attribute the problem? (Check all that apply to your child.)

___ My child is easily frustrated.

___ There are too many distractions.

___ My child is tired/unable to focus.

___ My child resents having to work at home.

___ Homework directions are not clear.

___ The assignment is too hard.

Other _____

11. Does your child have organizational problems related to homework? (Check all that apply to your child.)

___ My child doesn't realize there is a homework assignment.

___ My child forgets to write the assignment down.

___ My child forgets to bring home books or materials.

___ My child completes homework but forgets to turn it in or loses track of it.

Other _____

12. What resources do you have at home to assist your child in doing homework? (Check all that apply.)

___ A quiet place to work

___ Dictionary

___ Internet access

___ An adult with time to help

13. How involved are you in your child's homework? (Check all that apply to you.)

___ I don't get involved in my child's homework.

___ I check to see that my child's homework is done.

___ I have corrected my child's mistakes on homework.

___ I have completed homework for my child just to get it done.

___ I sometimes have trouble helping my child because I don't understand the directions.

___ I sometimes have trouble helping my child because I don't understand the material.

___ I'm not sure *how much* I should help my child with homework.

___ I have occasionally prohibited my child from doing homework because it interfered with sleep or family time.

Other _____

14. What could teachers do to make the homework process better and less stressful for your child? (Check all that you agree with.)

___ Stop giving homework altogether.

___ Give less homework.

___ Make homework optional or for extra credit.

___ Make sure the child has written down the homework assignment.

___ Make sure the child understands the homework.

___ Provide a copy of the textbook to keep at home.

___ Give clearer instructions to students about homework.

___ Set a maximum amount of time the child should work on each assignment.

___ Prioritize assignments in case the child does not have time to complete all homework.

___ Give assignments further in advance of the due date.

___ Give students more than one day to complete assignments.

___ Make assignments accessible from home via a homework phone line or website.

___ Allow parents to call the teacher at home when necessary.

___ Let parents know how homework is graded and what percentage of the total quarter grade it accounts for.

___ Give parents guidance on *how* to help with homework and *how much* to help.

___ Provide a cover sheet that encourages parents to communicate about homework in writing to the teacher.

APPENDIX E
Homework Policy Planning Template

Homework policies are best designed with input from all stake-holders—teachers, parents, and students—and should reflect the unique needs of the school community. No single policy would be appropriate for all schools.

However, to assist educators in crafting homework policies, it may be helpful to consider what a robust homework policy might include. Below are suggestions for components of such a policy and examples of typical policy statements. These are by no means all-inclusive, but they should provide a starting point for policy development.

Possible Homework Policy Component	Examples of Possible Policy Statements
Rationale or guiding principles	• Carefully planned homework can complement classroom learning. • Well-designed homework strengthens students' academic skills. • It is important to respect a balance between schoolwork and family life. • The physical and mental health of our students is important.

Possible Homework Policy Component	Examples of Possible Policy Statements
Definition of homework	Homework is defined as any task assigned by teachers to be completed outside the classroom.
Definition of purposes of homework or types of homework	Five purposes of homework are • Prelearning. • Diagnosis. • Checking for understanding. • Practice. • Processing.
Definition of effective homework tasks	Effective homework is • Meaningful. • Connected to learning goals. • Developmentally appropriate (provides necessary scaffolding, is of age-appropriate difficulty). • Differentiated to accommodate learner needs.
Homework as feedback	• Homework should provide feedback to the teacher about student understanding and progress. • All homework should receive feedback. • Teachers should provide feedback about homework in a timely manner.

Possible Homework Policy Component	Examples of Possible Policy Statements
Amount of homework assigned/time limits	• There is no requirement for teachers to give homework. • Homework should not be assigned to kindergarten students. • The maximum amount of homework to be assigned should not exceed 10 minutes per grade level per night. Broader categories may also be created, such as the following: — Grades 1–3: reading homework only, 10–20 minutes per night — Grades 4–6: maximum of 30 minutes of homework per night — Grades 7–9: maximum of 70 minutes of homework per night — Grades 10–12: maximum of 120 minutes of homework per night
Weighting of homework in the grade	The following are various options for weighting homework that schools may consider: • Homework may not be counted in the grade but will be reported in the Work Habits section of the report card. • Homework may count a maximum of 5 percent in the quarter grade. • Homework may count a maximum of 10 percent in the quarter grade. • Formative practice homework does not count in the grade, but summative assignments (such as research papers) may count within the percentage limit.

Possible Homework Policy Component	Examples of Possible Policy Statements
Weekend homework	• Homework may be assigned Monday through Thursday. • Homework may not be assigned on weekends. • No homework will be due on Mondays.
Holiday or summer homework	• Homework may not be assigned on legal or religious holidays. • Homework may not be assigned over school vacations. • No homework will be due the first two days after a school vacation. • Homework may not be assigned over summer break, although suggestions for summer enrichment may be provided.
Economic equity	Purchasing supplies needed to complete homework is optional. The school will furnish homework supplies to any families financially unable to.
Homework support	If students are unable to complete homework at home, a homework support program will be provided at the school.

Calgary Roman Catholic School District Number 1 Administrative Procedures Manual

The following homework policy is one of the most comprehensive I have seen and should be a helpful resource for buildings or districts interested in developing their own policy. It was created cooperatively by administrators, teachers, and parents. It goes beyond most homework policies to delineate roles and responsibilities of teachers, students, parents, and administrators. The excerpt from the district's supporting document provides further guidance for teachers and parents regarding differentiation, extended absences, and incomplete work.

Homework: Administrative Procedure 364

Background

The district recognizes meaningful, carefully planned homework can support student success and be a complementary part of a student's overall learning program. The district also recognizes:

- The potential impact of homework on family life;

- The role homework may play in supporting students' self-confidence as a successful learner;
- The benefit of a district-wide, balanced, reasonable approach to homework.

The complexity of the topic of homework also requires conversation and cooperation at the school and classroom level to provide details, to clarify expectations, and to support student success with homework assignments.

This administrative procedure is further supported by related specifics as outlined in the Appendix.

Definition

Homework is "any task assigned by teachers intended for students to carry out during non-instructional hours" (Canadian Council on Learning, *A Systematic Review of Literature Examining the Impact of Homework on Academic Achievement*, 2009, p. 5).

Procedures

1. Types of Homework

For the purpose of this administrative procedure four types of homework are identified: Practice, Completion, Enrichment, and Projects.

1.1 Practice:

1.1.1 Practice homework reviews and reinforces skills and concepts taught during instructional time.

1.2 Completion:

1.2.1 Completion homework is work assigned during the school day that was not finished in a reasonable amount of time. This may include, but is not limited to, a written story or completing a set of questions. In situations where the majority of students have been unable to complete an assignment, additional class time is to be provided before it is assigned for homework.

1.3 Enrichment:

    1.3.1 Enrichment homework extends the learning be-yond curriculum expectations through such activ-ities as completing research related to a student's area of interest or undertaking an independent activity agreed upon with the teacher, potentially for extra credit.

1.4 Projects:

    1.4.1 Project homework relates to the curriculum and occurs when additional time outside of the school day is required to complete an activity or task assignment. Project homework may involve a small group of students who share the work of completing the project.

    1.4.2 When assigning a project for homework, it is particularly important for teachers to pay careful attention to how projects are differentiated for student success. Teachers must also supply clear marking criteria for students outlining all parts of the project and must make students/parents/legal guardians aware that purchasing of supplies for project homework is optional. Projects are to avoid placing any financial burden on parents/legal guardians and students. Generally, group project homework is not recommended in elemen-tary or junior high grades due to the challenges inherent in coordinating time among families.

While reading and writing are usually part of all homework assignments, it is also important to bear in mind that reading and other activities such as journal writing, recreational read-ing, vocabulary games, not assigned for mandatory completion by teachers are part of daily life and are not considered to be homework.

2. Guiding Principles

2.1 In designing homework for students, teachers must apply the following guiding principles:

    2.1.1 Ensure homework is purposeful and meaningful;

2.1.2 Plan and differentiate assignments in order to ensure students are able to complete homework independently or with minimal support;

2.1.3 Consider and be sensitive to the impact of homework on family life and balance the benefits of homework with respect for the value of family time;

2.1.4 Ensure students and parents/legal guardians are aware of and encouraged to use strategies for communicating challenges students may face in successfully completing homework;

2.1.5 When working with older students, seek their input into the structure of homework that best supports their learning and success;

2.1.6 Strive to identify interesting, engaging learning tasks for homework assignments;

2.1.7 Cooperate and coordinate homework assignments with other staff to identify best practices related to homework as a complement to learning and to avoid potential overload for the student at any one time.

2.2 The positive impact of homework relies upon student engagement, their success with completing their assignments and the ability of teachers to design assignments matched to students' learning needs. Differentiating homework assignments to meet this goal reflects the perspective that successful use of homework to support learning is not dependent upon the amount of time taken with homework but the degree to which it engages students, connects to the students' individual abilities, and links to the work undertaken in class.

3. Holidays and Weekends

3.1 In addition to consideration of homework types and the need for careful design of homework tasks, the district recognizes the importance of family time, the value of celebrating religious traditions, and the need to balance homework with other demands.

3.2 It is therefore recommended, and supported by stake-holders, that teachers refrain from assigning homework over long weekends or holidays. Since regular weekends are often filled with many family demands, discretion is to be used to ensure homework over regular weekends is no more than what might be normally assigned on a school night. Homework is also to be differentiated to reflect varying student needs.

3.3 In the case of older students, Grade 4 and up, it is important to recognize students may elect to use weekends for study and homework completion in order to balance busy week nights with homework responsibilities. For details please review the Appendix.

4. Recommended Times

To recognize the importance of personal and family time, it is recommended teachers use the following guidelines related to the quantity of homework.

4.1 The amount of homework assigned to students is to be differentiated according to age, developmental stage, and grade level along a continuum from lower to upper elementary, elementary to junior high, and junior high school to high school. At all levels, the time a student spends on homework may vary, and individual student needs and capacity are always to be considered.

4.2 Keeping in mind that the first grade in each divisional range below is to reflect time at the low end of the scale, with a gradual extension at the upper end of the division to the higher time range, the recommended time guidelines are:

4.3.1 Kindergarten to Grade 3

Occasional 5–10 minutes of homework per week.

4.3.2 Grades 4 to 6

Maximum of 30 minutes of homework per school night.

4.3.3 Grades 7 to 9

Maximum of 60 minutes of homework per school night.

4.3.4   Grades 10 to 12

Maximum of 120 minutes of homework per school night.

4.3   Additional explanation related to each of these grade levels is provided in the Appendix that accompanies this administrative procedure, *Supporting Implementation of Administrative Procedure 364*. Expectations and recommendations related to incomplete homework as well as the evaluation of homework are also included in the Appendix.

5. Roles and Responsibilities

Since student learning and success are shared responsibilities, teachers, parents/legal guardians, students, and school administrators all have important roles and responsibilities related to the completion of homework.

5.1   Teachers

Teachers have a responsibility to:

5.1.1   Maximize instruction during school hours by using strategies such as differentiated assessment and instruction;

5.1.2   Make every effort to differentiate expectations when homework is assigned;

5.1.3   Ensure homework is used for review, practice, enrichment, or completion of work rather than to introduce concepts or provide instruction (Instruction must occur in the classroom.);

5.1.4   Prepare students to succeed with homework and support them to develop skills they need to complete homework successfully;

5.1.5   Implement appropriate and reasonable homework practices and continually review and assess those practices;

5.1.6   Utilize appropriate strategies to communicate homework assignments to students, as well as strategies for completing assignments. For example, student agendas, electronic means, etc.

5.1.7 Establish communication strategies for parents/ legal guardians and students in cases where the student encounters challenges in completing the homework;

5.1.8 Undertake appropriate professional development related to homework practices.

5.2 Parents/Legal Guardians

5.2.1 Parents/legal guardians are educational partners with teachers. Homework is one of the options parents/legal guardians have to support their child's learning. Homework provides parents/ legal guardians with opportunities to:

5.2.1.1 Encourage and supervise learning as students practice skills at home;

5.2.1.2 Deepen their understanding of how their child is doing;

5.2.1.3 Model the family's commitment to education;

5.2.1.4 Provide appropriate assistance.

5.2.2 A key parental/legal guardian's responsibility is to communicate to teachers concerns related to homework completion, circumstances where their children are experiencing difficulty with their homework, or if there are extenuating cir- cumstances that made it difficult for the student to complete an assignment as planned.

5.2.3 Since homework is designed to support learning and is not intended to provide instruction, parents/legal guardians are not required to take on the role of a professional teacher.

5.2.4 Although, from time to time, schools may provide resources for enrichment of students, parents/ legal guardians are encouraged to take advantage of community resources to support enriched learning opportunities for their children (the public library, science centres, art galleries, museums, etc.).

5.2.5 Parents/legal guardians who wish to significantly modify homework expectations for their children are encouraged to meet with teachers and, when appropriate, school administration, to discuss the details of a homework plan to meet the student's needs.

5.3 Students

5.3.1 Students have a responsibility to do their best in completing assignments.

5.3.2 Students are also to be encouraged by their teacher and parents/legal guardians to share challenges that they encounter with homework, to develop an understanding of how homework benefits their learning and to provide feedback, reflective of their development level, related to the success of homework in supporting their learning.

5.4 School Administration

5.4.1 Homework is a complex topic which requires conversation and cooperation to develop specific details and processes that will meet school and individual student needs. Annually, principals must initiate the development or review of homework plans and procedures for their school. This must include input from parents/legal guardians, students, teachers, and other district personnel, if appropriate. On an ongoing basis, principals must monitor the consistent use of the school's plans and procedures for homework.

5.4.2 It is imperative that principals communicate the school homework plans and procedures through a variety of means including, but not limited to, websites, newsletters, letters to parents/legal guardians, and School Council meetings.

5.4.3 Principals have a responsibility to ensure students, teachers, parents/legal guardians, and School Council are aware of the district's homework administrative procedure. They also have a role in supporting teachers, parents/legal guardians, and students to find solutions to homework issues as well as in planning and coordinating professional development related to homework for their staff.

5.4.4   In collaboration with staff, principals are encouraged to organize and deliver professional development opportunities related to homework.

Appendix: Supporting Implementation of Administrative Procedure 364

This Appendix is intended as a resource to which teachers and administrators may refer for specific information related to implementation of the district's Homework Administrative Procedure 364.[*]

Differentiated Homework

The following guidelines related to the quantity of homework are recommended and recognize the importance of personal and family time:

- The amount of homework assigned to students is to be differentiated according to age, developmental stage, and grade level along a continuum from lower to upper elementary, elementary to junior high, and junior high school to high school;
- At all levels, the time a student spends on homework may vary and individual student needs and capacity is to be considered;
- Parents/legal guardians are to be aware of the process to use if their child experiences challenges with homework.

To further support consistency across the district in relation to homework, the following time-related guidelines are suggested. When using the guidelines, it is important to keep in mind that the same homework assignment may require different amounts of time to complete depending on each student's abilities and skills. There is also to be an awareness that English language learning students, students with diverse needs, or

---

[*] This is an excerpt from the Appendix for Supporting Implementation of Administrative Procedure 364.

students preparing for an exam may require a different amount of time to complete homework.

Time Guidelines Considerations

Keeping in mind that the first grade in each division is to reflect time at the low end of the scale, with a gradual extension at the upper end of the division to the higher time range, the recommended guidelines for each division are:

Kindergarten–Grade 3

- Occasional 5–10 minutes of homework per week.
- Formal assigned homework at kindergarten to Grade 3 levels is not recommended. Teachers may suggest and provide resources to support early learning activities such as reading, visits to community resources or interactive activities to develop skills. Completion of these learning opportunities is optional.
- Guidance from teachers to support parents/legal guardians to maximize regular family activities that support learning such as bedtime reading, meaningful writing to complete day-to-day tasks, enhancement of language through family events, and other community-based learning opportunities is encouraged. In Grade 3, limited amounts of formal homework may be introduced to reflect increased student maturity and independence.

Grades 4 to 6

- Maximum of 30 minutes of homework per school night.
- Various types of meaningful homework are introduced and may be assigned by teachers keeping in mind the balance of family time, the focus on supporting individual student success, the need to differentiate homework assignments, types and quantity, and the academic needs/abilities of the student.
- Since students are just beginning to develop skills needed to complete homework, it is recommended that teachers provide guidance and instruction related to areas such as:

- What to do if you encounter a problem finishing homework;
- How to manage time in relation to homework;
- Strategies for working independently, etc.

Grades 7 to 9

- Maximum of 60 minutes of homework per school night.
- The completion and management of homework tasks supports junior high students to take increasing responsibility for their learning. Since junior high students have many teachers, it is important for the school and teachers to identify and implement strategies to coordinate homework across the subject areas in order to avoid overloading at any one time.
- Consideration of the approach towards homework during examination time by all staff and subject teachers is important to allow students sufficient study and review time.

Grades 10 to 12

- Maximum of 120 minutes of homework per school night.
- Since high school students are young adults who may be required to undertake independent work as employees or as students at the post-secondary education level, they are to take increasing responsibility for managing and completing homework assignments. Teachers will work with students to meet the students' academic goals while at the same time designing homework to be meaningful and to reflect the students' realities at home.

Homework During Extended Absences

Homework has severe limitations as a strategy to compensate for missed classroom instruction due to absences related to holidays scheduled during regular school times. Since provision of instruction and ongoing, immediate follow-up are key components of successful use of homework to support learning, teachers shall not be expected to provide make-up assignments for students away on holidays. In such cases, it is recommended students read, practice math, maintain a journal, or create a photo record of their trip.

In certain circumstances, junior and senior high school students are encouraged to talk to their teachers about work missed so they can adequately prepare for assessments where there may be no flexibility to reschedule. Examples are the Provincial Achievement Tests, Diploma or International Baccalaureate exams.

For extended absences due to unexpected circumstances such as illness or a death in the family, parents/legal guardians are encouraged to contact the teacher to discuss available instructional options.

Incomplete Homework

Teachers are encouraged to work with parents/legal guardians and students in making up incomplete homework assignments. The teacher's first response to incomplete homework is to explore the reasons it was not completed. For example, was the homework too difficult, was there a lack of student understanding, were there exceptional circumstances? This opportunity for reflection and review may lead to different assignments, further explanations, or the provision of other resources to support the student.

As with all components of student learning, incomplete homework is to be communicated to parents/legal guardians verbally, in writing, and/or on the appropriate component of the report card:

- Learning skills (elementary);
- Work habits (junior high);
- General comments (senior high).

Removing a student from a subject or course to complete homework is inappropriate.

Evaluation of Homework

While teachers have flexibility in determining if a homework assignment will count towards a student's academic grade, collaboration at the grade, subject, and school level to develop consistent guidelines and practices related to when and how homework assignments are graded is important.

Prior to deducting marks for incomplete or poorly done homework, it is important for teachers to determine that the student clearly understood what was required, knew the concepts involved, and had the capacity necessary to complete the homework.

Homework assignments may be used by teachers to determine the next steps in teaching and learning. Homework, together with other forms of assessment, may also support the development of a better learner profile of a student's understanding of curriculum outcomes. While it is possible for some of the homework to be evaluated and marked, it is not a requirement or expectation that any homework be counted towards an academic grade.

Source: Copyright 2016 by Calgary Catholic School District. Reprinted with permission.

References

Abeles, V. (2015). *Beyond measure: Rescuing an overscheduled, overtested, underestimated generation.* New York: Simon and Schuster.

Allington, R. L. (2005). Ideology is still trumping evidence. *Phi Delta Kappan, 86*(6), 462.

American Psychological Association. (2014). *Stress in America: Are teens adopting adults' stress habits?* Washington, DC: Author.

American Psychological Association. (2015). How much math, science homework is too much? *Education Digest, 81*(2), 16–17.

Anderson, M. (2016). *Learning to choose, choosing to learn: The key to student motivation and achievement.* Alexandria, VA: ASCD.

Andrade, H. (2007–2008). Self-assessment through rubrics. *Educational Leadership, 65*(4), 60–63.

Azzam, A. M. (2014). Motivated to learn: A conversation with Daniel Pink. *Educational Leadership, 72*(1), 12–17.

Baker, D. P., & LeTendre, G. K. (2005). *National differences, global similarities: World culture and the future of schooling.* Stanford, CA: Stanford University Press.

Bas, G., Senturk, C., & Cigerci, F. (2017). Homework research and academic achievement: A meta-analytic review of research. *Issues in Educational Research, 27*(1), 31–50.

Bassok, D., Latham, S., & Rorem, A. (2016). Is kindergarten the new first grade? *AERA Open, 1*(4), 1–31.

Begley, S. (1998, March 30). Homework doesn't help. *Newsweek,* 50–51.

Bennett, C. A. (2017). "Most won't do it!" Examining homework as a structure for learning in a diverse middle school. *American Secondary Education, 45*(2), 22–38.

Bennett, S., & Kalish, N. (2006). *The case against homework: How homework is hurting our children and what we can do about it.* New York: Crown Publishers.

Bergmann, J. (2017). *Solving the homework problem by flipping the learning.* Alexandria, VA: ASCD.

Billingsley, C. (2014). Welcome to the genius hour. *AMLE Magazine.* Retrieved from https://www.amle.org/BrowsebyTopic/WhatsNew/WNDet/TabId/270/ArtMID/888/ArticleID/445/Welcome-to-the-Genius-Hour.aspx

Boorstin, J. (2014). High-tech tutoring: Big media, big start-ups & big money. *Media Money.* Retrieved from https://www.cnbc.com/2014/08/29/high-tech-tutoring-big-media-big-start-ups-big-money.html

Brookhart, S. M. (2007–2008). Feedback that fits. *Educational Leadership, 65*(4), 54–59.

Brookhart, S. M. (2017). *How to use grading to improve learning.* Alexandria, VA: ASCD.

Bryan, T., & Burstein, K. (2004). Improving homework completion and academic performance: Lessons from special education. *Theory into Practice, 43*(3), 213–219.

Buell, J. (2004). *Closing the book on homework: Enhancing public education and freeing family time.* Philadelphia: Temple University Press.

Carr, N. S. (2013). Increasing the effectiveness of homework for all learners in the inclusive classroom. *School Community Journal, 23*(1), 169–182.

CBS News. (2016, September 26). *Growing number of elementary schools now homework-free.* Retrieved from https://www.cbsnews.com/news/many-elementary-students-schooling-now-homework-free/

Chappuis, J. (2014). Thoughtful assessment with the learner in mind. *Educational Leadership, 71*(6), 20–26.

Christopher, S. (2007–2008). Homework: A few practice arrows. *Educational Leadership, 65*(4), 74–75.

Collins, K., & Bempechat, J. (2017). *No more mindless homework.* Portsmouth, NH: Heinemann.

Connors, N. A. (1991). *Homework: A new direction.* Columbus, OH: National Middle School Association.

Cool, V., & Keith, T. Z. (1991). Testing a model of school learning: Direct and indirect effects on academic achievement. *Contemporary Educational Psychology, 16,* 28–44.

Cooper, H. (1989a). *Homework.* White Plains, NY: Longman.

Cooper, H. (1989b). Synthesis of research on homework. *Educational Leadership, 47*(3), 85–91.

Cooper, H. (1994). *The battle over homework: An administrator's guide to setting sound and effective policies.* Thousand Oaks, CA: Corwin.

Cooper, H. (2001). *The battle over homework: Common ground for administrators, teachers, and parents* (2nd ed.). Thousand Oaks, CA: Corwin.

Cooper, H. (2007). *The battle over homework: Common ground for administrators, teachers, and parents* (3rd ed.). Thousand Oaks, CA: Corwin.

Cooper, H. (2016, September 2). Yes, teachers should give homework—the benefits are many. *The News & Observer.* Retrieved from http://www.newsobserver.com/opinion/op-ed/article99527192.html

Cooper, H., Lindsay, J. L., Nye, B., & Greathouse, S. (1998). Relationships among attitudes about homework, amount of homework assigned and completed, and student achievement. *Journal of Educational Psychology, 90*(1), 70–83.

Cooper, H., Robinson, J. C., & Patall, E. A. (2006). Does homework improve academic achievement? A synthesis of research, 1987–2003. *Review of Educational Research, 76*(1), 1–62.

Cooper, H., & Valentine, J. C. (2001). Using research to answer practical questions about homework. *Educational Psychologist, 36*(3), 143–153.

Corno, L. (1996). Homework is a complicated thing. *Educational Researcher, 25*(8), 27–30.

Corno, L., & Xu, J. (2004). Homework as the job of childhood. *Theory into Practice, 43*(3), 227–233.

Cushman, K. (2010a). *Fires in the mind: What kids can tell us about motivation and mastery.* San Francisco: Jossey-Bass.

Cushman, K. (2010b). Show us what homework is *for. Educational Leadership, 68*(1), 74–78.

Cushman, K. (2014). Conditions for motivated learning. *Phi Delta Kappan, 95*(8), 18–22.

Darling-Hammond, L., & Ifill-Lynch, O. (2006). If they'd only do their work! *Educational Leadership, 63*(5), 8–13.

Depka, E. (2015). *Bringing homework into focus: Tools and tips to enhance practices, design, and feedback.* Bloomington, IN: Solution Tree.

Dovey, D. (2018, April 17). Weight problems in children might be caused by not sleeping enough. *Newsweek.* Retrieved from http://www.newsweek.com/childhood-obesity-sleep-deprivation-overweight-kids-889886

Dueck, M. (2014). *Grading smarter, not harder: Assessment strategies that motivate kids and help them learn.* Alexandria, VA: ASCD.

Dunn, R., & Honigsfeld, A. (2013). Learning styles: What we know and what we need. *Educational Forum, 77*(2), 225–232.

Dweck, C. A. (2007). *Mindset: The new psychology of success.* New York: Ballantine Books.

Eaton, D. K., McKnight-Eily, L. R., Lowry, R., Perry, G. S., Presley-Cantrell, L., & Croft, J. B. (2010, April). Prevalence of insufficient, borderline, and optimal hours of sleep among high school students—United States, 2007. *Journal of Adolescent Health, 46*(4), 399–401.

Eisner, E. W. (2003–2004). Preparing for today and tomorrow. *Educational Leadership, 61*(4), 6–11.

Elkind, D. (1981). *The hurried child: Growing up too fast too soon.* Philadelphia: Da Capo Press.

Elkind, D. (2006). *The hurried child: Growing up too fast too soon* (25th anniversary ed.). Philadelphia: Da Capo Press.

Elkind, D. (2007). *The power of play: Learning what comes naturally.* Philadelphia: Da Capo Press.

Epstein, J. L., & Van Voorhis, F. L. (2001). More than minutes: Teachers' roles in designing homework. *Educational Psychologist, 36*(3), 181–193.

Eren, O., & Henderson, D. J. (2011). Are we wasting our children's time giving them more homework? *Economics of Education Review, 30*(5), 950–961.

Fan, H., Xu, J., Cai, Z., He, J., & Fan, X. (2017). Homework and students' achievement in math and science: A 30-year meta-analysis, 1986–2015. *Educational Research Review, 20*, 35–54.

Ferlazzo, L. (2011). Involvement or engagement? *Educational Leadership, 68*(8), 10–14.

Fernández-Alonso, R., Suárez-Álvarez, J., & Muñiz, J. (2015). Adolescents' homework performance in mathematics and science: Personal factors and teaching practices. *Journal of Educational Psychology, 107*(4), 1075–1085.

Floyd, J. (2016, August 25). Sorry, parents, your child probably doesn't have too much homework. *Dallas News.* Retrieved from https://www.dallasnews.com/opinion/commentary/2016/08/25/sorry-parents-child-probably-much-homework

Fry, R., & Kochhar, R. (2016, May 12). The shrinking middle class in U.S. metropolitan areas: 6 key findings. *Fact Tank: News in the Numbers.* Pew Research Center. Retrieved from http://www.pewresearch.org/fact-tank/2016/05/12/us-middle-class-metros-takeaways/

Galloway, M., Conner, J., & Pope, D. (2013). Non-academic effects of homework in privileged, high-performing high schools. *Journal of Experimental Education, 81*(4), 490–510.

Gardner, H. (1999). *Intelligence reframed: Multiple intelligences for the 21st century.* New York: Simon and Schuster.

Gill, B., & Schlossman, S. (1996). A sin against childhood: Progressive education and the crusade to abolish homework, 1897–1941. *American Journal of Education, 105*(1), 27–66.

Gill, B., & Schlossman, S. (2000). The lost cause of homework reform. *American Journal of Education, 109*(1), 27–36.

Gill, B. P., & Schlossman, S. L. (2004). Villain or savior? The American discourse on homework, 1850–2003. *Theory into Practice, 43*(3), 174–181.

Ginsburg, K. R. (2007). The importance of play in promoting healthy child development and maintaining strong parent-child bonds. *Pediatrics, 119*(1), 182–191.

Goldberg, K. (2007, April). *The homework trap.* Paper presented at the annual meeting of the American Educational Research Association, Chicago.

Goldberg, K. (2012). *The homework trap: How to save the sanity of parents, students and teachers*. Haddon Heights, NJ: Wyndmoor Press.

Greenfeld, K. T. (2013, October). My daughter's homework is killing me. *The Atlantic*. Retrieved from https://www.theatlantic.com/magazine/archive/2013/10/my-daughters-homework-is-killing-me/309514/

Guskey, T. R. (2003). How classroom assessments improve learning. *Educational Leadership, 52*(2), 14–20.

Guskey, T. R., & Anderman, E. M. (2008). Students at bat. *Educational Leadership, 66*(3), 8–14.

Guskey, T. R., & Jung, L. A. (2013). *Answers to essential questions about standards, assessments, grading, and reporting*. Thousand Oaks, CA: Corwin.

Hattie, J. (2009). *Visible learning*. London: Routledge.

Hattie, J. (2012). *Visible learning for teachers*. London: Routledge.

Hattie, J., & Yates, G. (2014). *Visible learning and the science of how we learn*. London: Routledge.

Hauser, C. (2016, August 24). As students return to school, debate about the amount of homework rages. *New York Times*. Retrieved from https://www.nytimes.com/2016/08/25/us/how-much-homework-is-too-much.html

Horsley, M., & Walker, R. (2013). *Reforming homework: Practices, learning and policy*. Melbourne, Australia: Palgrave Macmillan.

Huffington, A. (2014). *Thrive: The third metric to redefining success and creating a life of well-being, wisdom, and wonder*. New York: Crown Publishing.

Jackson, R. R. (2018). *Never work harder than your students and other principles of great teaching* (2nd ed.). Alexandria, VA: ASCD.

Jensen, E. (2000). *Brain-based learning*. San Diego, CA: The Brain Store.

Jensen, E. (2013). How poverty affects classroom engagement. *Educational leadership, 70*(8), 24–30.

Kallick, B., & Zmuda, A. (2017). *Students at the center: Personalized learning with habits of mind*. Alexandria, VA: ASCD.

Keith, T. Z. (1982). Time spent on homework and high school grades: A large-sample path analysis. *Journal of Educational Psychology, 74*(2), 248–253.

Keith, T. Z., & Cool, V. A. (1992). Testing models of school learning: Effects of quality instruction, motivation, academic coursework, and homework on academic achievement. *School Psychology Quarterly, 7*(3), 207–226.

Kohn, A. (1999). *Punished by rewards: The trouble with gold stars, incentive plans, A's, praise, and other bribes* (2nd ed.). New York: Houghton Mifflin.

Kohn, A. (2000). *The case against standardized testing: Raising the scores, ruining the schools*. Portsmouth, NH: Heinemann.

Kohn, A. (2004, September 15). The cult of rigor and the loss of joy. *Education Week*, pp. 35–36.

Kohn, A. (2006). *The homework myth: Why our kids get too much of a bad thing.* Cambridge, MA: Da Capo Press.

Kohn, A. (2011). The case against grades. *Educational Leadership, 69*(3), 28–33.

Kohn, A. (2015). *Schooling beyond measure and other unorthodox essays about education.* Portsmouth, NH: Heinemann.

Kralovec, E., & Buell, J. (2000). *The end of homework: How homework disrupts families, overburdens children, and limits learning.* Boston: Beacon Press.

Lahey, J. (2015). *The gift of failure: How the best parents learn to let go so their children can succeed.* New York: HarperCollins.

Lawrence, L. (2015, May 10). Do kids today have too much homework? *Christian Science Monitor.* Retrieved from https://www.csmonitor.com/USA/Society/2015/0510/Do-kids-today-have-too-much-homework

Levine, M. (2008). *The price of privilege: How parental pressure and material advantage are creating a generation of disconnected and unhappy kids.* New York: HarperCollins.

Levine, M. (2003). *The myth of laziness.* New York: Simon and Schuster.

Lin-Siegler, X., Dweck, C. S., & Cohen, G. L. (2016). Instructional interventions that motivate classroom learning. *Journal of Educational Psychology, 108*(3), 295–299.

Louv, R. (2005). *Last child in the woods: Saving our children from nature deficit disorder.* Chapel Hill, NC: Algonquin Books of Chapel Hill.

Louv, R. (2009–2010). Do our kids have nature-deficit disorder? *Educational Leadership, 67*(4), 24–30.

Lythcott-Haims, J. (2015). *How to raise an adult: Break free of the overparenting trap and prepare your kids for success.* New York: Henry Holt.

Maltese, A. V., Tai, R. H., & Fan, X. (2012). When is homework worth the time? Evaluating the association between homework and achievement in high school science and math. *High School Journal, 96*(1), 52–72.

Manninen, J. L. (2014). Teaching perseverance through differentiated homework. *Mathematics Teaching in the Middle School, 19*(8), 502–504.

Marzano, R. J. (2010). When practice makes perfect . . . sense. *Educational Leadership, 68*(3), 81–83.

Marzano, R. J., & Pickering, D. J. (2007). The case for and against homework. *Educational Leadership, 64*(6), 74–79.

Marzano, R. J., Pickering, D. J., & Pollock, J. E. (2001). *Classroom instruction that works: Research-based strategies for increasing student achievement.* Alexandria, VA: ASCD.

Milteer, R. M., & Ginsburg, K. R. (2012). The importance of play in promoting healthy child development and maintaining strong parent-child bond: Focus on children in poverty. *Pediatrics, 129*(1), e204–e213.

National Commission on Excellence in Education. (1983). *A nation at risk: The imperative for educational reform.* Washington, DC: Author.

National Governors Association Center for Best Practices (NGA Center) & Council of Chief State School Officers (CCSSO). (2010). *Common Core State Standards*. Washington, DC: Author.

National Sleep Foundation. (2014). *2014 Sleep in America poll: Sleep in the modern family*. Arlington, VA: Author.

Neason, A. (2017, January). Does homework help? *Education Update*. Alexandria, VA: ASCD.

Newman, C. (2017, February 16). Economic inequality in the U.S.: How bad is it, and why is it growing? *UVA Today*. Retrieved from https://www.news.virginia.edu/content/economic-inequality-us-how-bad-it-and-why-it-growing

Norton, J. (2013, September 23). Homework: Is there any point? *Christian Science Monitor*. Retrieved from https://www.csmonitor.com/The-Culture/Family/Modern-Parenthood/2013/0923/Homework-Is-there-any-point

Núñez, J. C., Suárez, N., Rosário, P., Vallejo, G., Cerezo, R., & Valle, A. (2015). Teachers' feedback on homework, homework-related behaviors, and academic achievement. *Journal of Educational Research, 108*(3), 204–216.

O'Connor, K. (2007). *A repair kit for grading: 15 fixes for broken grades*. Portland, OR: Educational Testing Service.

O'Connor, K. (2013). *The school leader's guide to grading*. Bloomington, IN: Solution Tree.

Organisation for Economic Co-operation and Development. (2015). *Does homework perpetuate inequalities in education?* Retrieved from www.oecd.org/pisa/pisa-2015-results-in-focus.pdf

Past, R. J. (2006). Homework that helps. *Principal Leadership, 7*(1), 8–9.

Perkins-Gough, D. (2006). Accelerating the learning of low achievers. *Educational Leadership, 63*(5), 88–90.

Pink, D. H. (2009). *Drive: The surprising truth about what motivates us*. New York: Riverhead Books.

Pope, D. (2001). *"Doing school": How we are creating a generation of stressed out, materialistic, and miseducated students*. New Haven, CT: Yale University Press.

Pope, D. C. (2005, April). Help for stressed students. *Educational Leadership, 62*(7), 33–37.

Pope, D. (2010). Beyond "doing school": From "stressed-out" to "engaged in learning." *Education Canada, 50*(1), 4–8.

Popham, W. J. (2008). *Transformative assessment*. Alexandria, VA: ASCD.

Porter, E. (2015, March 25). Relying on tests in grading the teacher. *New York Times*, p. B1.

Postman, N., & Weingartner, C. (1969). *Teaching as a subversive activity*. New York: Delacorte Press.

Pressman, R. M., Sugarman, D. B., Nemon, M. L., Desjartals, J., Owens, J. A., & Schettini-Evans, A. (2015). Homework and family stress: With consideration of parents' self-confidence, educational level, and cultural background. *American Journal of Family Therapy, 43*(4), 297–313.

Raebeck, B. (1992). *Transforming middle schools: A guide to whole-school change.* Lancaster, PA: Technomic.

Ratnesar, R. (1999, January 25). The homework ate my family. *Time,* 55–63.

Reardon, S. F. (2013). The widening income achievement gap. *Educational leadership, 70*(8), 10–16.

Rebora, A. (2006, February 8). Homework unburdened. *Education Week Teacher.* Retrieved from https://www.edweek.org/tm/articles/2006/02/08/0201trends_homework.html

Rebora, A. (2017). Perspectives: Personal matters. *Educational Leadership, 74*(6), 7.

Robbins, A. (2006). *The overachievers: The secret lives of driven kids.* New York: Hachette Books.

Rosenfeld, A., & Wise, N. (2000). *The overscheduled child: Avoiding the hyper-parenting trap.* New York: St. Martin's Griffin.

Rosenworcel, J. (2014, December 5). How to close the "homework gap." *Miami Herald.* Retrieved from http://www.miamiherald.com/opinion/op-ed/article4300806.html

Rothstein, R. (2004). *Class and schools: Using social, economic, and educational reform to close the black-white achievement gap.* New York: Teachers College Press.

Rothstein, R. (2010, October 14). How to fix our schools. *EPI Issue Brief #286.* Economic Policy Institute.

Sagor, R. (2008). Cultivating optimism in the classroom. *Educational Leadership, 65*(6), 26–31.

Schimmer, T. (2012). *Ten things that matter from assessment to grading.* Toronto, Canada: Pearson.

Schrobsdorff, S. (2016, October 27). Teen depression and anxiety: Why the kids are not alright. *Time,* 44–51. Retrieved from http://time.com/magazine/us/4547305/november-7th-2016-vol-188-no-19-u-s/

Spencer, K. (2017, April 25). Never mind the students; homework divides parents. *New York Times.* Retrieved from https://www.nytimes.com/2017/04/25/nyregion/homework-ban-new-york-city-schools.html

Spencer, K. (2018, April 4). Homework therapists' job: Help solve math problems, and emotional ones. *New York Times.* Retrieved from https://www.nytimes.com/2018/04/04/nyregion/homework-therapists-tutoring-counseling-new-york.html

Stahl, K. (2017, June 12). Do homework-burning parties send the wrong message? *POPSUGAR.* Retrieved from www.popsugar.com/moms/43614030

Stiggins, R. (2007). Assessment through the student's eyes. *Educational Leadership, 64*(8), 22–26.

Suitts, S. (2016). Students facing poverty: The new majority. *Educational Leadership, 74*(3), 36–40.

Taffel, R. (2001). *The second family.* New York: St. Martin's Press.

Taylor, J. (2007). *Motivating the uncooperative student: Redeeming discouragement and attitude problems.* Monmouth, OR: ADD Plus.

Tomlinson, C. A. (2009). Learning profiles and achievement. *School Administrator, 66*(2), 28–34.

Tomlinson, C. A. (2014a). *The differentiated classroom: Responding to the needs of all learners* (2nd ed.). Alexandria, VA: ASCD.

Tomlinson, C. A. (2014b). The bridge between today's lesson and tomorrow's. *Educational Leadership, 71*(6), 10–14.

Tomporowski, P. D., Davis, C. L., Miller, P. H., & Naglieri, J. A. (2008, June). Exercise and children's intelligence, cognition, and academic achievement. *Educational Psychology Review, 20*(2), 111–131.

Trautwein, U., & Koller, O. (2003). The relationship between homework and achievement—still much of a mystery. *Educational Psychology Review, 15*(2), 115–145.

Trautwein, U., Koller, O., Schmitz, B., & Baumert, J. (2002). Do homework assignments enhance achievement? A multilevel analysis in 7th grade mathematics. *Contemporary Educational Psychology, 27,* 26–50.

Trautwein, U., Niggli, A., Schnyder, I., & Ludtke, O. (2009). Between-teacher differences in homework assignments and the development of students' homework effort, homework emotions, and achievement. *Journal of Educational Psychology, 101*(1), 176–189.

U.S. Department of Education. (n.d.). *College- and career-ready standards.* Retrieved from https://www.ed.gov/k-12reforms/standards

Vatterott, C. (2003, January). There's something wrong with homework. *Principal, 64.*

Vatterott, C. (2005, October/November). Mom and Dad aren't taking algebra this year. *Our Children,* 4–7.

Vatterott, C. (2007). *Becoming a middle level teacher: Student-focused teaching of early adolescents.* New York: McGraw-Hill.

Vatterott, C. (2010). Five hallmarks of good homework. *Educational Leadership, 68*(1), 10–15.

Vatterott, C. (2014). Student-owned homework. *Educational Leadership, 71*(6), 39–42.

Vatterott, C. (2015). *Rethinking grading: Meaningful assessment for standards-based learning.* Alexandria, VA: ASCD.

Vatterott, C. (2017). One-size-doesn't-fit-all homework. *Educational Leadership, 74*(6), 34–39.

Watson, J. (2014, March 31). Should a school tell your kid they are fat? *Christian Science Monitor.* Retrieved from https://www.csmonitor.com/The-Culture/Family/2014/0331/Should-a-school-tell-your-kid-they-are-fat.

Weir, K. (2016). Is homework a necessary evil? *American Psychological Association Feature, 47*(3), 36. Retrieved from www.apa.org/monitor/2016/3/homework.aspx

Wildman, P. R. (1968). Homework pressures. *Peabody Journal of Education, 45*(4), 204.

Wiliam, D. (2016). The secret of effective feedback. *Educational Leadership, 73*(7), 10–15.

Williamson, R., & Johnston, J. H. (1999). Challenging orthodoxy: An emerging agenda for middle level reform. *Middle School Journal, 30*(4), 10–17.

Willingham, D., & Daniel, D. (2012). Teaching to what students have in common. *Educational Leadership, 69*(5), 16–21.

Willingham, D. T., Hughes, E. M., & Dobolyi, D. G. (2015). The scientific status of learning styles theory. *Teaching of Psychology, 42*(3), 266–271.

Wong, A. (2016, December 12). The American obsession with parenting. *The Atlantic.* Retrieved from https://www.theatlantic.com/family/archive/2016/12/the-american-obsession-with-parenting/510221/

Wright, J. (2006). Learning interventions for struggling students. *Education Digest, 71*(5), 35–39.

Index

Page references followed by an italicized *f* indicate information contained in figures.

About the Author

Dr. Cathy Vatterott is a professor of education at the University of Missouri–St. Louis, where she trains preservice middle school teachers. She is a former middle school and high school teacher and middle school principal. She is the author of numerous articles about education, including "Homework Myths" and "There's Something Wrong with Homework," and three other books: *Academic Success Through Empowering Students* (National Middle School Association, 1999), *Becoming a Middle Level Teacher: Student-Focused Teaching of Early Adolescents* (McGraw-Hill, 2007), and *Rethinking Grading: Meaningful Assessment for Standards-Based Learning* (ASCD, 2015).

She first became interested in homework in the late 1990s as the frustrated parent of a 5th grader with learning disabilities. Since then, she has presented her homework research to more than 12,000 educators and parents in the United States, Canada, and Europe. Dr. Vatterott is considered an international expert on the topic of K–12 homework and is often interviewed by media such as the *New York Times*, National Public Radio, *Time.com*, *USA Today*, BBC World News Service, the *Globe and Mail*, and the *Guardian*, as well as by writers from parenting magazines and educational organizations. She also serves on the advisory board for *Parents* magazine.

Some of her presentation materials and unpublished writings about homework can be found at her website, www.homeworklady.com. She can be reached through her website or at Vatterott@umsl.edu.

Related ASCD Resources

At the time of publication, the following resources were available (ASCD stock numbers appear in parentheses).

Print Products

Fast and Effective Assessment: How to Reduce Your Workload and Improve Student Learning by Glen Pearsall (#118002)

Flip Your Classroom: Reach Every Student in Every Class Every Day by Jonathan Bergmann and Aaron Sams (#112060)

Grading Smarter, Not Harder: Assessment Strategies That Motivate Kids and Help Them Learn by Myron Dueck (#114003)

Rethinking Grading: Meaningful Assessment for Standards-Based Learning by Cathy Vatterott (#115001)

Solving the Homework Problem by Flipping the Learning by Jonathan Bergmann (#117012)

For up-to-date information about ASCD resources, go to www.ascd.org. You can search the complete archives of *Educational Leadership* at www.ascd.org/el.

PD Online

Grading Smarter, Not Harder—PD Online Course (#PD16OC005M)

ASCD myTeachSource®

Download resources from a professional learning platform with hundreds of research-based best practices and tools for your classroom at http://myteachsource.ascd.org/.

For more information, send an e-mail to member@ascd.org; call 1-800-933-2723 or 703-578-9600; send a fax to 703-575-5400; or write to Information Services, ASCD, 1703 N. Beauregard St., Alexandria, VA 22311-1714 USA.

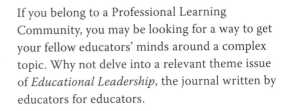

WHOLE CHILD
TENETS

The ASCD Whole Child approach is an effort to transition from a focus on narrowly defined academic achievement to one that promotes the long-term development and success of all children. Through this approach, ASCD supports educators, families, community members, and policymakers as they move from a vision about educating the whole child to sustainable, collaborative actions.

Rethinking Homework relates to the **healthy, engaged, supported,** and **challenged** tenets.

For more about the *ASCD Whole Child* approach, visit **www.ascd.org/wholechild.**

① HEALTHY
Each student enters school healthy and learns about and practices a healthy lifestyle.

② SAFE
Each student learns in an environment that is physically and emotionally safe for students and adults.

③ ENGAGED
Each student is actively engaged in learning and is connected to the school and broader community.

④ SUPPORTED
Each student has access to personalized learning and is supported by qualified, caring adults.

⑤ CHALLENGED
Each student is challenged academically and prepared for success in college or further study and for employment and participation in a global environment.